A Book of

German Lyrics

SELECTED AND EDITED WITH
NOTES AND VOCABULARY

BY
FRIEDRICH BRUNS

REVISED
EDITION

D. C. HEATH AND COMPANY
BOSTON

In Gratitude
TO
ALEXANDER RUDOLPH HOHLFELD
Who understood and encouraged my love for
German lyric poetry

PREFACE

In compiling this Anthology my aim has been not so much to acquaint the student with individual great poems as with the poets themselves. With this end in view I have made the selections as full and as varied as possible and included in the Notes short introductory sketches of the poets. Since the book is intended for the work of fourth and fifth semester German in College (or third and fourth year High School), pedagogic considerations imposed certain limitations not only as to individual poems but also as to poets. Thus I felt that I must exclude Novalis, Hölderlin, Brentano, Annette von Droste, Nietzsche and Dehmel. My standard of difficulty — aside from matters purely linguistic — was: Could a similar poem in English be read and appreciated by the same class of students? Moreover I tried out in a class of fourth semester German all poems that seemed to offer special difficulties and have made use of the experience thus acquired.

Some of my readers will undoubtedly be surprised at finding only two poems of Schiller included in the collection. May I point to the length of these two poems, 270 lines? Even to Goethe I have given only 362 lines. Why did I choose these two poems? The lighter lyric verse of Schiller is not representative of the poet nor would it have enriched the Anthology with a new note. *Das Lied von der Glocke* is too long for this small volume and is readily accessible in three different school editions. Schiller is at his best in his philosophical lyrics: as Goethe has said, in this field he is absolutely supreme. Poems like *Das Ideal und das Leben* or *Der Spaziergang* are far too difficult for our younger students. *Das verschleierte Bild zu Sais*, however, offers a philosophical problem which the younger mind can grasp without special training in philosophy. A few introductory remarks, such as I have given in the notes, will prepare the way. Both poems, furthermore, exemplify Schiller's ethical idealism. Certainly no other poems available at this stage could do more.

I have often been asked by teachers: How do you teach lyric poetry? An answer is found in my Notes to a number of the poems. The chief prerequisite is a warm love for the poets: nowhere is enthusiasm more contagious. A few introductory remarks will open the world of the poem to the student. The teacher must, of course, develop in the students their latent rhythmical sense both by example and precept. Aside from this lyric poetry teaches itself.

As to the use of the book I should suggest spending two or three weeks on one or two poets — I should begin with Goethe — and after that spend one hour a week for a semester or even a year. Some poems could be assigned for outside reading and then a group of poems be discussed in class.

On the whole I have limited myself to those poets that to-day stand out as preëminent. A possible exception is the once famous Rückert. I could not resist the temptation of including his *Aus der Jugendzeit*, a poem of consummate beauty, Rückert's one perfect lyric. Time has been relentless in its winnowing process.   But if Geibel, Wilhelm Müller and Bodenstedt have given way to Mörike, Keller and Hebbel, we assuredly have no reason for lament.   If this little book help to win in our schools for these three and for Storm, C. F. Meyer, and Liliencron the recognition they deserve, I shall feel richly repaid for this labor of love.

MADISON, WISCONSIN.

FRIEDRICH BRUNS.

PREFACE TO THE REVISED EDITION

More than a quarter of a century has passed since this little anthology set out on its way, and I am grateful for the kindly reception it has met.   In spite of the difficulties of the last decade its circulation increased, and this would seem to indicate that lip service (of which there was always plenty) to German lyric poetry has been replaced by a deeper appreciation.   Lyric poetry like music can reach depths in us the other arts do not touch.   The appeal is more direct, more immediate, more intimate.   I refer the reader to a beautiful essay by Ernst Wiechert: *Von den treuen Begleitern*.   Teachers may well refer their students to it.

In the main body of the book I have introduced only a few slight changes.   Heine's *Wo* has been replaced by *Der Asra*, the finest lyric of his *Romanzero*, and to make room for Keller's *Unter Sternen* it was necessary to delete Hebbel's *Der letzte Baum*.   These slight changes are, I believe, for the better.

I have added three poets: Dehmel, George, and Rilke. From the very start, friends asked about Dehmel. I am glad to yield a point here, and I trust that the eight poems I included will open up the way to the best of Dehmel. They should not be too difficult. And the same should hold true for the poems of George and Rilke that I have selected, five from each poet. After the student has become familiar with the selections from Goethe, Eichendorff, Mörike, Hebbel, and Meyer my brief introduction should clear the way to George and Rilke. If the teacher should desire a more adequate selection from these or any of the poets in this little volume I can now refer to my larger anthology: *Die Lese der deutschen Lyrik* (Crofts, New York. Second printing 1946). But for the real lover of the poets all anthologies are mere makeshifts. Sooner or later he will want to own his favorite poets in good editions. If my little *Book of German Lyrics* arouses this desire in its students I shall feel richly repaid.

F. B.

CONTENTS

Goethe

PAGE

1. Willkommen und Abschied 3
2. Mailied 4
3. Auf dem See 6
4. Heidenröslein 6
5. Wanderers Nachtlied 7
6. Ein gleiches 8
7. Hoffnung 8
8. Erinnerung 8
9. Gefunden 9
10. Mignon 9
11. Harfenspieler 10
12. Der König in Thule 11
13. Der Fischer 12
14. Erlkönig 13
15. Gesang der Geister über den Wassern 14
16. Grenzen der Menschheit 15
17. Lied des Türmers 17

Schiller

18. Die Kraniche des Ibykus 18
19. Das verschleierte Bild zu Sais 24

Uhland

20. Die Lerchen 28
21. Des Knaben Berglied 28
22. Schäfers Sonntagslied 29
23. Die Kapelle 30

                                                          PAGE
24. Morgenlied.   30
25. Frühlingsglaube.   31
26. Lob des Frühlings   31
27. Das Schwert   31
28. Die Rache   32
29. Der Wirtin Töchterlein   33
30. Der gute Kamerad   34
31. Taillefer   34
32. Des Sängers Fluch.   37

Eichendorff

33. Der frohe Wandersmann   40
34. Der Jäger Abschied   40
35. Nachts   41
36. Frühlingsdämmerung.   42
37. Elfe.   43
38. Abendlandschaft   43
39. Die Nacht   44
40. Sehnsucht   44
41. Das zerbrochene Ringlein   45
42. Frühe   46
43. Nachts   46
44. Mondnacht   47

Rückert

45. Aus der Jugendzeit   48

Heine

46. Die Grenadiere   50
47. In mein gar zu dunkles Leben   51
48. Ich weiß nicht, was soll es bedeuten   52
49. Du bist wie eine Blume   53
50. Auf Flügeln des Gesanges   53
51. Die Lotosblume ängstigt   54
52. Ein Fichtenbaum   55
53. Mein Liebchen, wir saßen beisammen   55

                                                        PAGE
54. Ein Jüngling liebt ein Mädchen   56
55. Dämmernd liegt der Sommerabend   56
56. Es fällt ein Stern herunter   57
57. Der Tod, das ist die kühle Nacht   57
58. Sag, wo ist dein schönes Liebchen   58
59. Frieden   58
60. Leise zieht durch mein Gemüt   60
61. Es war ein alter König   60
62. Es ziehen die brausenden Wellen   61
63. Es ragt ins Meer der Runenstein   61
64. In der Fremde   61
65. Der Asra   62

Platen

66. Das Grab im Busento   63
67. Im Wasser wogt die Lilie   64
68. Wie rafft' ich mich auf in der Nacht   64
69. Ich möchte, wann ich sterbe   65

Lenau

70. Bitte   66
71. Schilflied   66
72. Der Eichwald   67
73. Der Postillion   67
74. Die Drei   70
75. Der offene Schrank   71
76. Auf eine holländische Landschaft   72
77. Stimme des Regens   72
78. Herbst   73

Mörike

79. Um Mitternacht   74
80. Septembermorgen   74
81. Er ist's   75
82. In der Frühe   75
83. Der Feuerreiter   75

PAGE

84. Das verlassene Mägdlein 77
85. Lebewohl 78
86. Schön-Rohtraut 78
87. Auf eine Lampe 80
88. Gebet 80
89. Denk' es, o Seele 80

Hebbel

90. Nachtlied 82
91. Das Kind 82
92. Nachtgefühl 83
93. Gebet 84
94. Abendgefühl 85
95. Ich und du 85
96. Sommerbild 86
97. Herbstbild 86

Keller

98. An das Vaterland 87
99. Winternacht 88
100. Abendlied 88
101. Unter Sternen 89

Storm

102. Oktoberlied 91
103. Weihnachtslied 92
104. Sommermittag 92
105. Die Stadt 93
106. Über die Heide 94
107. Lucie 94
108. Eine Frühlingsnacht 95
109. April 96
110. Mai 97
111. Elisabeth 97
112. Frauenhand 98
113. Schließe mir die Augen beide 98

Meyer

PAGE

114. Liederseelen 99
115. Nachtgeräusche 99
116. Das tote Kind 100
117. Im Spätboot 100
118. Vor der Ernte 101
119. Der römische Brunnen 101
120. Neujahrsglocken 102
121. Säerspruch 102
122. Schnitterlied 103
123. Nach einem Niederländer 103
124. Eingelegte Ruder 104
125. Ewig jung ist nur die Sonne 104
126. Requiem 105
127. Abendwolke 105
128. Das Glöcklein 106
129. Die Bank des Alten 107

Liliencron

130. Die Musik kommt 108
131. Tod in Ähren 109
132. In Erinnerung 110
133. Wer weiß wo 110
134. Sommernacht 112
135. Meiner Mutter 112
136. Wiegenlied 112
137. Viererzug 113
138. Schöne Junitage 114

Dehmel

139. Der Arbeitsmann 115
140. Die stille Stadt 116
141. Dann 116
142. Manche Nacht 117
143. Nacht für Nacht 117
144. Befreit 118

		PAGE
145.	Gleichnis	118
146.	Hochsommerlied	119

George

147.	Die Spange	120
148.	Der Einsiedel	120
149.	Wir schreiten auf und ab	121
150.	Ihr tratet zu dem Herde	121
151.	Das Licht	122

Rilke

152.	Die armen Worte	123
153.	Der Panther	123
154.	Die Erblindende	124
155.	Du mußt das Leben nicht verstehen	125
156.	Widmung	125

NOTES	127
VOCABULARY	169
INDEX OF TITLES AND FIRST LINES	207

A BOOK OF GERMAN LYRICS

Ein kleines Lied

Ein kleines Lied, wie geht's nur an,
Daß man so lieb es haben kann,
Was liegt darin? Erzähle!

Es liegt darin ein wenig Klang,
Ein wenig Wohllaut und Gesang,
Und eine ganze Seele.

Marie von Ebner-Eschenbach.

A BOOK OF GERMAN LYRICS

Johann Wolfgang von Goethe

1. Willkommen und Abschied

Es schlug mein Herz, geschwind zu Pferde!
Es war getan, fast eh' gedacht;
Der Abend wiegte schon die Erde,
Und an den Bergen hing die Nacht;
Schon stand im Nebelkleid die Eiche,   5
Ein aufgetürmter Riese, da,
Wo Finsternis aus dem Gesträuche
Mit hundert schwarzen Augen sah.

Der Mond von einem Wolkenhügel
Sah kläglich aus dem Duft hervor;   10
Die Winde schwangen leise Flügel,
Umsausten schauerlich mein Ohr;
Die Nacht schuf tausend Ungeheuer,
Doch frisch und fröhlich war mein Mut:
In meinen Adern, welches Feuer!   15
In meinem Herzen, welche Glut!

Dich sah ich, und die milde Freude
Floß von dem süßen Blick auf mich;
Ganz war mein Herz an deiner Seite,
Und jeder Atemzug für dich.   20

Ein rosenfarbnes Frühlingswetter
Umgab das liebliche Gesicht,
Und Zärtlichkeit für mich — ihr Götter!
Ich hofft' es, ich verdient' es nicht!

25   Doch ach, schon mit der Morgensonne
Verengt der Abschied mir das Herz:
In deinen Küssen, welche Wonne!
In deinem Auge, welcher Schmerz!
Ich ging, du standst und sahst zur Erden,
30   Und sahst mir nach mit nassem Blick:
Und doch, welch Glück, geliebt zu werden!
Und lieben, Götter, welch ein Glück!

2. Mailied

Wie herrlich leuchtet
Mir die Natur!
Wie glänzt die Sonne!
Wie lacht die Flur!

5   Es dringen Blüten
Aus jedem Zweig,
Und tausend Stimmen
Aus dem Gesträuch,

Und Freud' und Wonne
10   Aus jeder Brust.
O Erd', o Sonne!
O Glück, o Lust!

O Lieb', o Liebe!
So golden schön,
Wie Morgenwolken   15
Auf jenen Höhn!

Du segnest herrlich
Das frische Feld,
Im Blütendampfe
Die volle Welt.   20

O Mädchen, Mädchen,
Wie lieb' ich dich!
Wie blinkt dein Auge!
Wie liebst du mich!

So liebt die Lerche   25
Gesang und Luft,
Und Morgenblumen
Den Himmelsduft,

Wie ich dich liebe
Mit warmem Blut,   30
Die du mir Jugend
Und Freud' und Mut

Zu neuen Liedern
Und Tänzen giebst.
Sei ewig glücklich,   35
Wie du mich liebst!

3. Auf dem See

Und frische Nahrung, neues Blut
Saug' ich aus freier Welt;
Wie ist Natur so hold und gut,
Die mich am Busen hält!
5 Die Welle wieget unsern Kahn
Im Rudertakt hinauf,
Und Berge, wolkig himmelan,
Begegnen unserm Lauf.

Aug', mein Aug', was sinkst du nieder?
10 Goldne Träume, kommt ihr wieder?
Weg, du Traum! so gold du bist;
Hier auch Lieb' und Leben ist.

Auf der Welle blinken
Tausend schwebende Sterne;
15 Weiche Nebel trinken
Rings die türmende Ferne;
Morgenwind umflügelt
Die beschattete Bucht,
Und im See bespiegelt
20 Sich die reifende Frucht.

4. Heidenröslein

Sah ein Knab' ein Röslein stehn,
Röslein auf der Heiden,
War so jung und morgenschön,
Lief er schnell, es nah zu sehn,
5 Sah's mit vielen Freuden.

Röslein, Röslein, Röslein rot,
Röslein auf der Heiden.

Knabe sprach: Ich breche dich,
Röslein auf der Heiden!
Röslein sprach: Ich steche dich,   10
Daß du ewig denkst an mich,
Und ich will's nicht leiden.
Röslein, Röslein, Röslein rot,
Röslein auf der Heiden.

Und der wilde Knabe brach   15
's Röslein auf der Heiden;
Röslein wehrte sich und stach,
Half ihm doch kein Weh und Ach,
Mußt' es eben leiden.
Röslein, Röslein, Röslein rot,   20
Röslein auf der Heiden.

5. Wandrers Nachtlied

Der du von dem Himmel bist,
Alles Leid und Schmerzen stillest,
Den, der doppelt elend ist,
Doppelt mit Erquickung füllest,
Ach, ich bin des Treibens müde!   5
Was soll all der Schmerz und Lust?
Süßer Friede,
Komm, ach, komm in meine Brust!

6. Ein gleiches

Über allen Gipfeln
Ist Ruh;
In allen Wipfeln
Spürest du
Kaum einen Hauch;
Die Vögelein schweigen im Walde.
Warte nur, balde
Ruhest du auch.

7. Hoffnung

Schaff', das Tagwerk meiner Hände,
Hohes Glück, daß ich's vollende!
Laß, o laß mich nicht ermatten!
Nein, es sind nicht leere Träume:
Jetzt nur Stangen, diese Bäume
Geben einst noch Frucht und Schatten.

8. Erinnerung

Willst du immer weiter schweifen?
Sieh, das Gute liegt so nah.
Lerne nur das Glück ergreifen,
Denn das Glück ist immer da.

9. Gefunden

Ich ging im Walde
So für mich hin,
Und nichts zu suchen,
Das war mein Sinn.

Im Schatten sah ich   5
Ein Blümchen stehn,
Wie Sterne leuchtend,
Wie Äuglein schön.

Ich wollt' es brechen,
Da sagt' es fein: 10
Soll ich zum Welken
Gebrochen sein?

Ich grub's mit allen
Den Würzlein aus,
Zum Garten trug ich's   15
Am hübschen Haus.

Und pflanzt' es wieder
Am stillen Ort;
Nun zweigt es immer
Und blüht so fort.   20

10. Mignon

Kennst du das Land, wo die Zitronen blühn,
Im dunkeln Laub die Goldorangen glühn,

Ein sanfter Wind vom blauen Himmel weht,
Die Myrte still und hoch der Lorbeer steht?
5 Kennst du es wohl?
                    Dahin! Dahin
Möcht' ich mit dir, o mein Geliebter, ziehn.

Kennst du das Haus? Auf Säulen ruht sein Dach,
Es glänzt der Saal, es schimmert das Gemach,
Und Marmorbilder stehn und sehn mich an:
10 Was hat man dir, du armes Kind, getan?
Kennst du es wohl?
                    Dahin! Dahin
Möcht' ich mit dir, o mein Beschützer, ziehn.

Kennst du den Berg und seinen Wolkensteg?
Das Maultier sucht im Nebel seinen Weg;
15 In Höhlen wohnt der Drachen alte Brut;
Es stürzt der Fels und über ihn die Flut.
Kennst du ihn wohl?
                    Dahin! Dahin
Geht unser Weg! o Vater, laß uns ziehn!

11. Harfenspieler

Wer nie sein Brot mit Tränen aß,
Wer nie die kummervollen Nächte
Auf seinem Bette weinend saß,
Der kennt euch nicht, ihr himmlischen Mächte.

5 Ihr führt ins Leben uns hinein,
Ihr laßt den Armen schuldig werden,
Dann überlaßt ihr ihn der Pein:
Denn alle Schuld rächt sich auf Erden.

12. Der König in Thule

Es war ein König in Thule,
Gar treu bis an das Grab,
Dem sterbend seine Buhle
Einen goldnen Becher gab.

Es ging ihm nichts darüber,   5
Er leert' ihn jeden Schmaus;
Die Augen gingen ihm über,
So oft er trank daraus.

Und als er kam zu sterben,
Zählt' er seine Städt' im Reich,   10
Gönnt' alles seinem Erben,
Den Becher nicht zugleich.

Er saß beim Königsmahle,
Die Ritter um ihn her,
Auf hohem Vätersaale   15
Dort auf dem Schloß am Meer.

Dort stand der alte Zecher,
Trank letzte Lebensglut
Und warf den heil'gen Becher
Hinunter in die Flut.   20

Er sah ihn stürzen, trinken
Und sinken tief ins Meer.
Die Augen täten ihm sinken,
Trank nie einen Tropfen mehr.

13. Der Fischer

Das Wasser rauscht', das Wasser schwoll,
Ein Fischer saß daran,
Sah nach dem Angel ruhevoll,
Kühl bis ans Herz hinan.
5 Und wie er sitzt und wie er lauscht,
Teilt sich die Flut empor:
Aus dem bewegten Wasser rauscht
Ein feuchtes Weib hervor.

Sie sang zu ihm, sie sprach zu ihm:
10 Was lockst du meine Brut
Mit Menschenwitz und Menschenlist
Hinauf in Todesglut?
Ach, wüßtest du, wie 's Fischlein ist
So wohlig auf dem Grund,
15 Du stiegst herunter, wie du bist,
Und würdest erst gesund.

Labt sich die liebe Sonne nicht,
Der Mond sich nicht im Meer?
Kehrt wellenatmend ihr Gesicht
20 Nicht doppelt schöner her?
Lockt dich der tiefe Himmel nicht,
Das feuchtverklärte Blau?
Lockt dich dein eigen Angesicht
Nicht her in ew'gen Tau?

25 Das Wasser rauscht', das Wasser schwoll,
Netzt' ihm den nackten Fuß;
Sein Herz wuchs ihm so sehnsuchtsvoll,
Wie bei der Liebsten Gruß.

Sie sprach zu ihm, sie sang zu ihm;
Da war's um ihn geschehn: 30
Halb zog sie ihn, halb sank er hin
Und ward nicht mehr gesehn.

14. Erlkönig

Wer reitet so spät durch Nacht und Wind?
Es ist der Vater mit seinem Kind;
Er hat den Knaben wohl in dem Arm,
Er faßt ihn sicher, er hält ihn warm.

„Mein Sohn, was birgst du so bang dein Gesicht?" —   5
„Siehst, Vater, du den Erlkönig nicht?
Den Erlenkönig mit Kron' und Schweif?" —
„Mein Sohn, es ist ein Nebelstreif."

„Du liebes Kind, komm, geh mit mir!
„Gar schöne Spiele spiel' ich mit dir;   10
„Manch bunte Blumen sind an dem Strand,
„Meine Mutter hat manch gülden Gewand." —

„Mein Vater, mein Vater, und hörest du nicht,
Was Erlkönig mir leise verspricht?" —
„Sei ruhig, bleibe ruhig, mein Kind;   15
In dürren Blättern säuselt der Wind." —

„Willst, feiner Knabe, du mit mir gehn?
„Meine Töchter sollen dich warten schön;
„Meine Töchter führen den nächtlichen Reihn
„Und wiegen und tanzen und singen dich ein." —   20

„Mein Vater, mein Vater, und siehst du nicht dort
Erlkönigs Töchter am düstern Ort?" —
„Mein Sohn, mein Sohn, ich seh' es genau:
Es scheinen die alten Weiden so grau." —

25 „Ich liebe dich, mich reizt deine schöne Gestalt;
„Und bist du nicht willig, so brauch' ich Gewalt." —
„Mein Vater, mein Vater, jetzt faßt er mich an!
Erlkönig hat mir ein Leids getan!" —

Dem Vater grauset's, er reitet geschwind,
30 Er hält in Armen das ächzende Kind,
Erreicht den Hof mit Mühe und Not;
In seinen Armen das Kind war tot.

15. Gesang der Geister über den Wassern

Des Menschen Seele
Gleicht dem Wasser:
Vom Himmel kommt es,
Zum Himmel steigt es,
5 Und wieder nieder
Zur Erde muß es,
Ewig wechselnd.

Strömt von der hohen,
Steilen Felswand
10 Der reine Strahl,
Dann stäubt er lieblich
In Wolkenwellen
Zum glatten Fels,

Und leicht empfangen,
Wallt er verschleiernd,   15
Leis rauschend
Zur Tiefe nieder.

Ragen Klippen
Dem Sturz entgegen,
Schäumt er unmutig   20
Stufenweise
Zum Abgrund.

Im flachen Bette
Schleicht er das Wiesental hin,
Und in dem glatten See   25
Weiden ihr Antlitz
Alle Gestirne.

Wind ist der Welle
Lieblicher Buhler;
Wind mischt vom Grund aus   30
Schäumende Wogen.

Seele des Menschen,
Wie gleichst du dem Wasser!
Schicksal des Menschen,
Wie gleichst du dem Wind!   35

16. Grenzen der Menschheit

Wenn der uralte
Heilige Vater
Mit gelassener Hand
Aus rollenden Wolken

5   Segnende Blitze
       Über die Erde sät,
       Küss' ich den letzten
       Saum seines Kleides,
       Kindliche Schauer
10   Treu in der Brust.

       Denn mit Göttern
       Soll sich nicht messen
       Irgend ein Mensch.
       Hebt er sich aufwärts
15   Und berührt
       Mit dem Scheitel die Sterne,
       Nirgends haften dann
       Die unsichern Sohlen,
       Und mit ihm spielen
20   Wolken und Winde.

       Steht er mit festen,
       Markigen Knochen
       Auf der wohlgegründeten
       Dauernden Erde:
25   Reicht er nicht auf,
       Nur mit der Eiche
       Oder der Rebe
       Sich zu vergleichen.

       Was unterscheidet
30   Götter von Menschen?
       Daß viele Wellen
       Vor jenen wandeln,
       Ein ewiger Strom:

Uns hebt die Welle,
Verschlingt die Welle, 35
Und wir versinken.

Ein kleiner Ring
Begrenzt unser Leben,
Und viele Geschlechter
Reihen sich dauernd 40
An ihres Daseins
Unendliche Kette.

17. Lied des Türmers

Zum Sehen geboren,
Zum Schauen bestellt,
Dem Turme geschworen,
Gefällt mir die Welt.

Ich blick' in die Ferne, 5
Ich seh' in der Näh'
Den Mond und die Sterne,
Den Wald und das Reh.

So seh' ich in allen
Die ewige Zier, 10
Und wie mir's gefallen,
Gefall' ich auch mir.

Ihr glücklichen Augen,
Was je ihr gesehn,
Es sei, wie es wolle, 15
Es war doch so schön!

Friedrich Schiller

18. Die Kraniche des Ibykus

Zum Kampf der Wagen und Gesänge,
Der auf Korinthus' Landesenge
Der Griechen Stämme froh vereint,
Zog Ibykus, der Götterfreund.
Ihm schenkte des Gesanges Gabe,
Der Lieder süßen Mund Apoll;
So wandert' er an leichtem Stabe
Aus Rhegium, des Gottes voll.

Schon winkt auf hohem Bergesrücken
Akrokorinth des Wandrers Blicken,
Und in Poseidons Fichtenhain
Tritt er mit frommem Schauder ein.
Nichts regt sich um ihn her; nur Schwärme
Von Kranichen begleiten ihn,
Die fernhin nach des Südens Wärme
In graulichtem Geschwader ziehn.

„Seid mir gegrüßt, befreundte Scharen,
Die mir zur See Begleiter waren;
Zum guten Zeichen nehm' ich euch,
Mein Los, es ist dem euren gleich:
Von fern her kommen wir gezogen
Und flehen um ein wirtlich Dach.
Sei uns der Gastliche gewogen,
Der von dem Fremdling wehrt die Schmach!"

Und munter fördert er die Schritte, 25
Und sieht sich in des Waldes Mitte;
Da sperren auf gedrangem Steg,
Zwei Mörder plötzlich seinen Weg.
Zum Kampfe muß er sich bereiten,
Doch bald ermattet sinkt die Hand, 30
Sie hat der Leier zarte Saiten,
Doch nie des Bogens Kraft gespannt.

Er ruft die Menschen an, die Götter,
Sein Flehen dringt zu keinem Retter;
Wie weit er auch die Stimme schickt, 35
Nichts Lebendes wird hier erblickt.
„So muß ich hier verlassen sterben,
Auf fremdem Boden, unbeweint,
Durch böser Buben Hand verderben,
Wo auch kein Rächer mir erscheint!" 40

Und schwer getroffen sinkt er nieder,
Da rauscht der Kraniche Gefieder;
Er hört, schon kann er nicht mehr sehn,
Die nahen Stimmen furchtbar krähn.
„Von euch, ihr Kraniche dort oben, 45
Wenn keine andre Stimme spricht,
Sei meines Mordes Klag' erhoben!"
Er ruft es, und sein Auge bricht.

Der nackte Leichnam wird gefunden,
Und bald, obgleich entstellt von Wunden, 50
Erkennt der Gastfreund in Korinth
Die Züge, die ihm teuer sind.

„Und muß ich so dich wiederfinden,
Und hoffte mit der Fichte Kranz
55   Des Sängers Schläfe zu umwinden,
Bestrahlt von seines Ruhmes Glanz!"

Und jammernd hören's alle Gäste,
Versammelt bei Poseidons Feste,
Ganz Griechenland ergreift der Schmerz,
60   Verloren hat ihn jedes Herz.
Und stürmend drängt sich zum Prytanen
Das Volk, es fodert seine Wut,
Zu rächen des Erschlagnen Manen,
Zu sühnen mit des Mörders Blut.

65   Doch wo die Spur, die aus der Menge,
Der Völker flutendem Gedränge,
Gelocket von der Spiele Pracht,
Den schwarzen Täter kenntlich macht?
Sind's Räuber, die ihn feig erschlagen?
70   Tat's neidisch ein verborgner Feind?
Nur Helios vermag's zu sagen,
Der alles Irdische bescheint.

Er geht vielleicht mit frechem Schritte
Jetzt eben durch der Griechen Mitte,
75   Und während ihn die Rache sucht,
Genießt er seines Frevels Frucht.
Auf ihres eignen Tempels Schwelle
Trotzt er vielleicht den Göttern, mengt
Sich dreist in jene Menschenwelle,
80   Die dort sich zum Theater drängt.

Denn Bank an Bank gedränget sitzen,
Es brechen fast der Bühne Stützen,
Herbeigeströmt von fern und nah',
Der Griechen Völker wartend da.
Dumpfbrausend wie des Meeres Wogen,   85
Von Menschen wimmelnd wächst der Bau
In weiter stets geschweiftem Bogen
Hinauf bis in des Himmels Blau.

Wer zählt die Völker, nennt die Namen,
Die gastlich hier zusammenkamen?   90
Von Kekrops' Stadt, von Aulis' Strand,
Von Phokis, vom Spartanerland,
Von Asiens entlegner Küste,
Von allen Inseln kamen sie,
Und horchen von dem Schaugerüste   95
Des Chores grauser Melodie,

Der, streng und ernst, nach alter Sitte
Mit langsam abgemeßnem Schritte
Hervortritt aus dem Hintergrund,
Umwandelnd des Theaters Rund.   100
So schreiten keine ird'schen Weiber!
Die zeugete kein sterblich Haus!
Es steigt das Riesenmaß der Leiber
Hoch über Menschliches hinaus.

Ein schwarzer Mantel schlägt die Lenden,   105
Sie schwingen in entfleischten Händen
Der Fackel düsterrote Glut,
In ihren Wangen fließt kein Blut.

Und wo die Haare lieblich flattern,
110   Um Menschenstirnen freundlich wehn,
Da sieht man Schlangen hier und Nattern
Die giftgeschwollnen Bäuche blähn.

Und schauerlich gedreht im Kreise,
Beginnen sie des Hymnus Weise,
115   Der durch das Herz zerreißend dringt,
Die Bande um den Sünder schlingt.
Besinnungraubend, herzbetörend
Schallt der Erinnyen Gesang.
Er schallt, des Hörers Mark verzehrend,
120   Und duldet nicht der Leier Klang:

„Wohl dem, der frei von Schuld und Fehle
Bewahrt die kindlich reine Seele!
Ihm dürfen wir nicht rächend nahn,
Er wandelt frei des Lebens Bahn.
125   Doch wehe, wehe, wer verstohlen
Des Mordes schwere Tat vollbracht!
Wir heften uns an seine Sohlen,
Das furchtbare Geschlecht der Nacht.

„Und glaubt er fliehend zu entspringen,
130   Geflügelt sind wir da, die Schlingen
Ihm werfend um den flücht'gen Fuß,
Daß er zu Boden fallen muß.
So jagen wir ihn ohn' Ermatten,
Versöhnen kann uns keine Reu',
135   Ihn fort und fort bis zu den Schatten,
Und geben ihn auch dort nicht frei."

So singend, tanzen sie den Reigen,
Und Stille, wie des Todes Schweigen,
Liegt überm ganzen Hause schwer,
Als ob die Gottheit nahe wär'.   140
Und feierlich nach alter Sitte
Umwandelnd des Theaters Rund
Mit langsam abgemeßnem Schritte,
Verschwinden sie im Hintergrund.

Und zwischen Trug und Wahrheit schwebet   145
Noch zweifelnd jede Brust und bebet,
Und huldiget der furchtbarn Macht,
Die richtend im Verborgnen wacht,
Die, unerforschlich, unergründet,
Des Schicksals dunkeln Knäuel flicht,   150
Dem tiefen Herzen sich verkündet,
Doch fliehet vor dem Sonnenlicht.

Da hört man auf den höchsten Stufen
Auf einmal eine Stimme rufen:
„Sieh da, sieh da, Timotheus,   155
Die Kraniche des Ibykus!" —
Und finster plötzlich wird der Himmel,
Und über dem Theater hin
Sieht man in schwärzlichtem Gewimmel
Ein Kranichheer vorüberziehn.   160

„Des Ibykus!" — Der teure Name
Rührt jede Brust mit neuem Grame,
Und wie im Meere Well' auf Well',
So läuft's von Mund zu Munde schnell:

165 „Des Ibykus? den wir beweinen?
Den eine Mörderhand erschlug?
Was ist's mit dem? was kann er meinen?
Was ist's mit diesem Kranichzug?" —

Und lauter immer wird die Frage,
170 Und ahnend fliegt's mit Blitzesschlage
Durch alle Herzen: „Gebet acht,
Das ist der Eumeniden Macht!
Der fromme Dichter wird gerochen,
Der Mörder bietet selbst sich dar —
175 Ergreift ihn, der das Wort gesprochen,
Und ihn, an den's gerichtet war!"

Doch dem war kaum das Wort entfahren,
Möcht' er's im Busen gern bewahren;
Umsonst! der schreckenbleiche Mund
180 Macht schnell die Schuldbewußten kund.
Man reißt und schleppt sie vor den Richter,
Die Szene wird zum Tribunal,
Und es gestehn die Bösewichter,
Getroffen von der Rache Strahl.

19. Das verschleierte Bild zu Sais

Ein Jüngling, den des Wissens heißer Durst
Nach Sais in Ägypten trieb, der Priester
Geheime Weisheit zu erlernen, hatte
Schon manchen Grad mit schnellem Geist durcheilt;
5 Stets riß ihn seine Forschbegierde weiter,

Und kaum besänftigte der Hierophant
Den ungeduldig Strebenden. „Was hab' ich,
Wenn ich nicht alles habe?" sprach der Jüngling.
„Gibt's etwa hier ein Weniger und Mehr?
Ist deine Wahrheit wie der Sinne Glück   10
Nur eine Summe, die man größer, kleiner
Besitzen kann und immer doch besitzt?
Ist sie nicht eine einz'ge, ungeteilte?
Nimm Einen Ton aus einer Harmonie,
Nimm Eine Farbe aus dem Regenbogen,   15
Und alles, was dir bleibt, ist nichts, solang'
Das schöne All der Töne fehlt und Farben."

Indem sie einst so sprachen, standen sie
In einer einsamen Rotonde still,
Wo ein verschleiert Bild von Riesengröße   20
Dem Jüngling in die Augen fiel. Verwundert
Blickt er den Führer an und spricht: „Was ist's,
Das hinter diesem Schleier sich verbirgt?" —
„Die Wahrheit", ist die Antwort. — „Wie?" ruft jener,
„Nach Wahrheit streb' ich ja allein, und diese   25
Gerade ist es, die man mir verhüllt?"

„Das mache mit der Gottheit aus", versetzt
Der Hierophant. „Kein Sterblicher, sagt sie,
Rückt diesen Schleier, bis ich selbst ihn hebe.
Und wer mit ungeweihter, schuld'ger Hand   30
Den heiligen, verbotnen früher hebt,
Der, spricht die Gottheit" — „Nun?" — „Der sieht
    die Wahrheit."
„Ein seltsamer Orakelspruch! Du selbst,
Du hättest also niemals ihn gehoben?"

35   „Ich? — Wahrlich nicht! Und war auch nie dazu
     Versucht." — „Das faß' ich nicht.   Wenn von der Wahrheit
     Nur diese dünne Scheidewand mich trennte" —
     „Und ein Gesetz", fällt ihm sein Führer ein,
     „Gewichtiger, mein Sohn, als du es meinst,
40   Ist dieser dünne Flor — für deine Hand
     Zwar leicht, doch zentnerschwer für dein Gewissen."

     Der Jüngling ging gedankenvoll nach Hause;
     Ihm raubt des Wissens brennende Begier
     Den Schlaf, er wälzt sich glühend auf dem Lager
45   Und rafft sich auf um Mitternacht.   Zum Tempel
     Führt unfreiwillig ihn der scheue Tritt.
     Leicht ward es ihm, die Mauer zu ersteigen,
     Und mitten in das Innre der Rotonde
     Trägt ein beherzter Sprung den Wagenden.

50   Hier steht er nun, und grauenvoll umfängt
     Den Einsamen die lebenlose Stille,
     Die nur der Tritte hohler Widerhall
     In den geheimen Grüften unterbricht.
     Von oben durch der Kuppel Öffnung wirft
55   Der Mond den bleichen, silberblauen Schein,
     Und furchtbar wie ein gegenwärt'ger Gott
     Erglänzt durch des Gewölbes Finsternisse
     In ihrem langen Schleier die Gestalt.

     Er tritt hinan mit ungewissem Schritt;
60   Schon will die freche Hand das Heilige berühren,
     Da zuckt es heiß und kühl durch sein Gebein
     Und stößt ihn weg mit unsichtbarem Arme.
     Unglücklicher, was willst du tun? So ruft
     In seinem Innern eine treue Stimme.

Verfuchen den Allheiligen willft du? 65
Kein Sterblicher, fprach des Orakels Mund
Rückt diefen Schleier, bis ich felbft ihn hebe.
Doch, fetzte nicht derfelbe Mund hinzu:
Wer diefen Schleier hebt, foll Wahrheit fchauen?
„Sei hinter ihm, was will! Ich heb' ihn auf." 70
Er ruft's mit lauter Stimm'. „Ich will fie fchauen."
      Schauen!
Gellt ihm ein langes Echo fpottend nach.

Er fpricht's und hat den Schleier aufgedeckt.
„Nun", fragt ihr, „und was zeigte fich ihm hier?" 75
Ich weiß es nicht. Befinnungslos und bleich,
So fanden ihn am andern Tag die Priefter
Am Fußgeftell der Ifis ausgeftreckt.
Was er allda gefehen und erfahren,
Hat feine Zunge nie bekannt. Auf ewig 80
War feines Lebens Heiterkeit dahin,
Ihn riß ein tiefer Gram zum frühen Grabe.
„Weh' dem", dies war fein warnungsvolles Wort,
Wenn ungeftüme Frager in ihn drangen,
„Weh' dem, der zu der Wahrheit geht durch Schuld, 85
Sie wird ihm nimmermehr erfreulich fein!"

Ludwig Uhland

20. Die Lerchen

Welch ein Schwirren, welch ein Flug?
Sei willkommen, Lerchenzug!
Jene streift der Wiese Saum,
Diese rauschet durch den Baum.

5   Manche schwingt sich himmelan,
Jauchzend auf der lichten Bahn;
Eine, voll von Liedeslust,
Flattert hier in meiner Brust.

21. Des Knaben Berglied

Ich bin vom Berg der Hirtenknab',
Seh' auf die Schlösser all herab;
Die Sonne strahlt am ersten hier,
Am längsten weilet sie bei mir;
5   Ich bin der Knab' vom Berge!

Hier ist des Stromes Mutterhaus,
Ich trink' ihn frisch vom Stein heraus;
Er braust vom Fels in wildem Lauf,
Ich fang' ihn mit den Armen auf;
10   Ich bin der Knab' vom Berge!

Der Berg, der ist mein Eigentum,
Da ziehn die Stürme rings herum;
Und heulen sie von Nord und Süd,
So überschallt sie doch mein Lied:
Ich bin der Knab' vom Berge! 15

Sind Blitz und Donner unter mir,
So steh' ich hoch im Blauen hier;
Ich kenne sie und rufe zu:
Laßt meines Vaters Haus in Ruh'!
Ich bin der Knab' vom Berge! 20

Und wann die Sturmglock' einst erschallt,
Manch Feuer auf den Bergen wallt,
Dann steig' ich nieder, tret' ins Glied
Und schwing' mein Schwert und sing' mein Lied:
Ich bin der Knab' vom Berge! 25

22. Schäfers Sonntagslied

Das ist der Tag des Herrn!
Ich bin allein auf weiter Flur;
Noch e i n e Morgenglocke nur,
Nun Stille nah und fern.

Anbetend knie' ich hier. 5
O süßes Graun, geheimes Wehn,
Als knieten viele ungesehn
Und beteten mit mir!

Der Himmel nah und fern,
Er ist so klar und feierlich, 10
So ganz, als wollt' er öffnen sich.
Das ist der Tag des Herrn!

23. Die Kapelle

Droben stehet die Kapelle,
Schauet still ins Tal hinab,
Drunten singt bei Wies' und Quelle
Froh und hell der Hirtenknab'.

5 Traurig tönt das Glöcklein nieder,
Schauerlich der Leichenchor;
Stille sind die frohen Lieder,
Und der Knabe lauscht empor.

Droben bringt man sie zu Grabe,
10 Die sich freuten in dem Tal;
Hirtenknabe, Hirtenknabe!
Dir auch singt man dort einmal.

24. Morgenlied

Noch ahnt man kaum der Sonne Licht,
Noch sind die Morgenglocken nicht
Im finstern Tal erklungen.

Wie still des Waldes weiter Raum!
5 Die Vöglein zwitschern nur im Traum,
Kein Sang hat sich erschwungen.

Ich hab' mich längst ins Feld gemacht
Und habe schon dies Lied erdacht
Und hab' es laut gesungen.

25. Frühlingsglaube

Die linden Lüfte sind erwacht,
Sie säuseln und weben Tag und Nacht,
Sie schaffen an allen Enden.
O frischer Duft, o neuer Klang!
Nun, armes Herze, sei nicht bang!   5
Nun muß sich alles, alles wenden.

Die Welt wird schöner mit jedem Tag,
Man weiß nicht, was noch werden mag,
Das Blühen will nicht enden.
Es blüht das fernste, tiefste Tal;   10
Nun, armes Herz, vergiß der Qual!
Nun muß sich alles, alles wenden.

26. Lob des Frühlings

Saatengrün, Veilchenduft,
Lerchenwirbel, Amselschlag,
Sonnenregen, linde Luft!

Wenn ich solche Worte singe,
Braucht es dann noch großer Dinge,   5
Dich zu preisen, Frühlingstag?

27. Das Schwert

Zur Schmiede ging ein junger Held,
Er hatt' ein gutes Schwert bestellt;
Doch als er's wog in freier Hand,
Das Schwert er viel zu schwer erfand.

5   Der alte Schmied den Bart sich streicht:
„Das Schwert ist nicht zu schwer noch leicht,
Zu schwach ist Euer Arm, ich mein';
Doch morgen soll geholfen sein."

„Nein, heut, bei aller Ritterschaft!
10   Durch meine, nicht durch Feuers Kraft."
Der Jüngling spricht's, ihn Kraft durchdringt,
Das Schwert er hoch in Lüften schwingt.

28. Die Rache

Der Knecht hat erstochen den edeln Herrn,
Der Knecht wär' selber ein Ritter gern.

Er hat ihn erstochen im dunkeln Hain
Und den Leib versenket im tiefen Rhein.

5   Hat angeleget die Rüstung blank,
Auf des Herren Roß sich geschwungen frank.

Und als er sprengen will über die Brück',
Da stutzet das Roß und bäumt sich zurück.

Und als er die güldnen Sporen ihm gab,
10   Da schleudert's ihn wild in den Strom hinab.

Mit Arm, mit Fuß er rudert und ringt,
Der schwere Panzer ihn niederzwingt.

29. Der Wirtin Töchterlein

Es zogen drei Bursche wohl über den Rhein,
Bei einer Frau Wirtin, da kehrten sie ein:

„Frau Wirtin, hat Sie gut Bier und Wein?
Wo hat Sie Ihr schönes Töchterlein?"

„Mein Bier und Wein ist frisch und klar.   5
Mein Töchterlein liegt auf der Totenbahr'."

Und als sie traten zur Kammer hinein,
Da lag sie in einem schwarzen Schrein.

Der erste, der schlug den Schleier zurück
Und schaute sie an mit traurigem Blick: 10

„Ach, lebtest du noch, du schöne Maid!
Ich würde dich lieben von dieser Zeit."

Der zweite deckte den Schleier zu
Und kehrte sich ab und weinte dazu:

„Ach, daß du liegst auf der Totenbahr'!   15
Ich hab' dich geliebet so manches Jahr."

Der dritte hub ihn wieder sogleich
Und küßte sie an den Mund so bleich:

„Dich lieb' ich immer, dich lieb' ich noch heut
Und werde dich lieben in Ewigkeit."   20

30. Der gute Kamerad

Ich hatt' einen Kameraden,
Einen bessern findst du nit.
Die Trommel schlug zum Streite,
Er ging an meiner Seite
5   In gleichem Schritt und Tritt.

Eine Kugel kam geflogen;
Gilt's mir oder gilt es dir?
Ihn hat es weggerissen,
Er liegt mir vor den Füßen,
10   Als wär's ein Stück von mir.

Will mir die Hand noch reichen,
Derweil ich eben lad':
„Kann dir die Hand nicht geben;
Bleib du im ew'gen Leben
15   Mein guter Kamerad!"

31. Taillefer

Normannenherzog Wilhelm sprach einmal:
„Wer singet in meinem Hof und in meinem Saal?
Wer singet vom Morgen bis in die späte Nacht
So lieblich, daß mir das Herz im Leibe lacht?"

5 „Das ist der Taillefer, der so gerne singt
Im Hofe, wenn er das Rad am Brunnen schwingt,
Im Saale, wann er das Feuer schüret und facht,
Wann er abends sich legt und wann er morgens erwacht."

Der Herzog sprach: „Ich hab' einen guten Knecht,
Den Taillefer; der dienet mir fromm und recht,   10
Er treibt mein Rad und schüret mein Feuer gut
Und singet so hell; das höhet mir den Mut."

Da sprach der Taillefer: „Und wär' ich frei,
Viel besser wollt' ich dienen und singen dabei.
Wie wollt' ich dienen dem Herzog hoch zu Pferd!   15
Wie wollt' ich singen und klingen mit Schild und mit Schwert!"

Nicht lange, so ritt der Taillefer ins Gefild
Auf einem hohen Pferde mit Schwert und mit Schild.
Des Herzogs Schwester schaute vom Turm ins Feld;
Sie sprach: „Dort reitet, bei Gott, ein stattlicher Held."   20

Und als er ritt vorüber an Fräuleins Turm,
Da sang er bald wie ein Lüftlein, bald wie ein Sturm.
Sie sprach: „Der singet, das ist eine herrliche Lust;
Es zittert der Turm, und es zittert mein Herz in der Brust."

Der Herzog Wilhelm fuhr wohl über das Meer,   25
Er fuhr nach Engelland mit gewaltigem Heer.
Er sprang vom Schiffe, da fiel er auf die Hand;
„Hei," rief er, „ich fass' und ergreife dich, Engelland!"

Als nun das Normannenheer zum Sturme schritt,
Der edle Taillefer vor den Herzog ritt: 30
„Manch Jährlein hab' ich gesungen und Feuer geschürt,
Manch Jährlein gesungen und Schwert und Lanze gerührt.

„Und hab' ich Euch gedient und gesungen zu Dank,
Zuerst als ein Knecht und dann als ein Ritter frank,

35 So laßt mich das entgelten am heutigen Tag,
   Vergönnet mir auf die Feinde den ersten Schlag!"

   Der Taillefer ritt vor allem Normannenheer
   Auf einem hohen Pferde mit Schwert und mit Speer;
   Er sang so herrlich, das klang über Hastingsfeld;
40 Von Roland sang er und manchem frommen Held.

   Und als das Rolandslied wie ein Sturm erscholl,
   Da wallete manch Panier, manch Herze schwoll,
   Da brannten Ritter und Mannen von hohem Mut;
   Der Taillefer sang und schürte das Feuer gut.

45 Dann sprengt' er hinein und führte den ersten Stoß,
   Davon ein englischer Ritter zur Erde schoß;
   Dann schwang er das Schwert und führte den ersten Schlag,
   Davon ein englischer Ritter am Boden lag.

   Normannen sahen's, die harrten nicht allzulang,
50 Sie brachen herein mit Geschrei und mit Schilderklang.
   Hei, sausende Pfeile, klirrender Schwerterschlag!
   Bis Harald fiel und sein trotziges Heer erlag.

   Herzog Wilhelm steckte sein Banner aufs blutige Feld,
   Inmitten der Toten spannt' er sein Gezelt;
55 Da saß er am Mahle, den goldnen Pokal in der Hand,
   Auf dem Haupte die Königskrone von Engelland:

   „Mein tapfrer Taillefer, komm! trink mir Bescheid!
   Du hast mir viel gesungen in Lieb' und in Leid;
   Doch heut im Hastingsfelde dein Sang und dein Klang,
60 Der tönet mir in den Ohren mein Leben lang."

32. Des Sängers Fluch

Es stand in alten Zeiten ein Schloß, so hoch und hehr,
Weit glänzt es über die Lande bis an das blaue Meer,
Und rings von duft'gen Gärten ein blütenreicher Kranz,
Drin sprangen frische Brunnen in Regenbogenglanz.

Dort saß ein stolzer König, an Land und Siegen reich,   5
Er saß auf seinem Throne so finster und so bleich;
Denn was er sinnt, ist Schrecken, und was er blickt, ist Wut,
Und was er spricht, ist Geißel, und was er schreibt, ist Blut.

Einst zog nach diesem Schlosse ein edles Sängerpaar,
Der ein' in goldnen Locken, der andre grau von Haar;   10
Der Alte mit der Harfe, der saß auf schmuckem Roß,
Es schritt ihm frisch zur Seite der blühende Genoß.

Der Alte sprach zum Jungen: „Nun sei bereit, mein Sohn!
Denk unsrer tiefsten Lieder, stimm an den vollsten Ton!
Nimm alle Kraft zusammen, die Lust und auch den Schmerz! 15
Es gilt uns heut, zu rühren des Königs steinern Herz."

Schon stehn die beiden Sänger im hohen Säulensaal,
Und auf dem Throne sitzen der König und sein Gemahl,
Der König furchtbar prächtig wie blut'ger Nordlichtschein,
Die Königin süß und milde, als blickte Vollmond drein.   20

Da schlug der Greis die Saiten, er schlug sie wundervoll,
Daß reicher, immer reicher der Klang zum Ohre schwoll;
Dann strömte himmlisch helle des Jünglings Stimme vor,
Des Alten Sang dazwischen wie dumpfer Geisterchor.

25 Sie singen von Lenz und Liebe, von sel'ger goldner Zeit,
Von Freiheit, Männerwürde, von Treu' und Heiligkeit,
Sie singen von allem Süßen, was Menschenbrust durchbebt,
Sie singen von allem Hohen, was Menschenherz erhebt.

Die Höflingsschar im Kreise verlernet jeden Spott,
30 Des Königs trotz'ge Krieger, sie beugen sich vor Gott;
Die Königin, zerflossen in Wehmut und in Lust,
Sie wirft den Sängern nieder die Rose von ihrer Brust.

„Ihr habt mein Volk verführet; verlockt ihr nun mein Weib?"
Der König schreit es wütend, er bebt am ganzen Leib;
35 Er wirft sein Schwert, das blitzend des Jünglings Brust
    durchdringt,
Draus statt der goldnen Lieder ein Blutstrahl hoch aufspringt.

Und wie vom Sturm zerstoben ist all der Hörer Schwarm.
Der Jüngling hat verröchelt in seines Meisters Arm;
Der schlägt um ihn den Mantel und setzt ihn auf das Roß,
40 Er bind't ihn aufrecht feste, verläßt mit ihm das Schloß.

Doch vor dem hohen Tore, da hält der Sängergreis,
Da faßt er seine Harfe, sie, aller Harfen Preis,
An einer Marmorsäule, da hat er sie zerschellt;
Dann ruft er, daß es schaurig durch Schloß und Gärten gellt:

45 „Weh euch, ihr stolzen Hallen! Nie töne süßer Klang
Durch eure Räume wieder, nie Saite noch Gesang,
Nein, Seufzer nur und Stöhnen und scheuer Sklavenschritt,
Bis euch zu Schutt und Moder der Rachegeist zertritt!

„Weh euch, ihr duft'gen Gärten im holden Maienlicht!
50 Euch zeig' ich dieses Toten entstelltes Angesicht,

Daß ihr darob verdorret, daß jeder Quell versiegt,
Daß ihr in künft'gen Tagen versteint, verödet liegt.

„Weh dir, verruchter Mörder! du Fluch des Sängertums!
Umsonst sei all dein Ringen nach Kränzen blut'gen Ruhms!
Dein Name sei vergessen, in ew'ge Nacht getaucht,   55
Sei wie ein letztes Röcheln in leere Luft verhaucht!"

Der Alte hat's gerufen, der Himmel hat's gehört,
Die Mauern liegen nieder, die Hallen sind zerstört;
Noch e i n e hohe Säule zeugt von verschwundner Pracht;
Auch diese, schon geborsten, kann stürzen über Nacht.   60

Und rings statt duft'ger Gärten ein ödes Heideland,
Kein Baum verstreuet Schatten, kein Quell durchdringt den
        Sand,
Des Königs Namen meldet kein Lied, kein Heldenbuch;
Versunken und vergessen! das ist des Sängers Fluch.

Joseph von Eichendorff

33. Der frohe Wandersmann

Wem Gott will rechte Gunst erweisen,
Den schickt er in die weite Welt;
Dem will er seine Wunder weisen
In Berg und Wald und Strom und Feld.

5 Die Trägen, die zu Hause liegen,
Erquicket nicht das Morgenrot;
Sie wissen nur von Kinderwiegen,
Von Sorgen, Last und Not um Brot.

Die Bächlein von den Bergen springen,
10 Die Lerchen schwirren hoch vor Lust,
Was sollt' ich nicht mit ihnen singen
Aus voller Kehl' und frischer Brust?

Den lieben Gott laß' ich nur walten;
Der Bächlein, Lerchen, Wald und Feld
15 Und Erd' und Himmel will erhalten,
Hat auch mein' Sach' aufs best' bestellt!

34. Der Jäger Abschied

Wer hat dich, du schöner Wald,
Aufgebaut so hoch da droben?

40

Wohl den Meister will ich loben,
So lang' noch mein' Stimm' erschallt.
Lebe wohl,   5
Lebe wohl, du schöner Wald!

Tief die Welt verworren schallt,
Oben einsam Rehe grasen,
Und wir ziehen fort und blasen,
Daß es tausendfach verhallt: 10
Lebe wohl,
Lebe wohl, du schöner Wald!

Banner, der so kühle wallt!
Unter deinen grünen Wogen
Hast du treu uns auferzogen,   15
Frommer Sagen Aufenthalt!
Lebe wohl,
Lebe wohl, du schöner Wald!

Was wir still gelobt im Wald,
Wollen's draußen ehrlich halten,   20
Ewig bleiben treu die Alten:
Deutsch Panier, das rauschend wallt,
Lebe wohl!
Schirm dich Gott, du schöner Wald!

35. Nachts

Ich stehe in Waldesschatten
Wie an des Lebens Rand,
Die Länder wie dämmernde Matten,
Der Strom wie ein silbern Band.

5   Von fern nur schlagen die Glocken
Über die Wälder herein,
Ein Reh hebt den Kopf erschrocken
Und schlummert gleich wieder ein.

Der Wald aber rühret die Wipfel
10   Im Traum von der Felsenwand.
Denn der Herr geht über die Gipfel
Und segnet das stille Land.

36. Frühlingsdämmerung

In der stillen Pracht,
In allen frischen Büschen und Bäumen
Flüstert's wie Träumen
Die ganze Nacht.
5   Denn über den mondbeglänzten Ländern
Mit langen weißen Gewändern
Ziehen die schlanken
Wolkenfrau'n wie geheime Gedanken,
Senden von den Felsenwänden
10   Hinab die behenden
Frühlingsgesellen, die hellen Waldquellen,
Die's unten bestellen
An die duft'gen Tiefen,
Die gerne noch schliefen.
15   Nun wiegen und neigen in ahnendem Schweigen
Sich alle so eigen
Mit Ähren und Zweigen,
Erzählen's den Winden,
Die durch die blühenden Linden

Vorüber den grasenden Rehen   20
Säuselnd über die Seen gehen,
Daß die Nixen verschlafen auftauchen
Und fragen,
Was sie so lieblich hauchen —
Wer mag es wohl sagen?   25

37. Elfe

Bleib bei uns! wir haben den Tanzplan im Tal
Bedeckt mit Mondesglanze,
Johanneswürmchen erleuchten den Saal,
Die Heimchen spielen zum Tanze.

Die Freude, das schöne leichtgläubige Kind,   5
Es wiegt sich in Abendwinden:
Wo Silber auf Zweigen und Büschen rinnt,
Da wirst du die schönste finden!

38. Abendlandschaft

Der Hirt bläst seine Weise,
Von fern ein Schuß noch fällt,
Die Wälder rauschen leise
Und Ströme tief im Feld.

Nur hinter jenem Hügel   5
Noch spielt der Abendschein —
O hätt' ich, hätt' ich Flügel,
Zu fliegen da hinein!

39. Die Nacht

Nacht ist wie ein stilles Meer,
Lust und Leid und Liebesklagen
Kommen so verworren her
In dem linden Wellenschlagen.

Wünsche wie die Wolken sind,
Schiffen durch die stillen Räume,
Wer erkennt im lauen Wind,
Ob's Gedanken oder Träume? —

Schließ' ich nun auch Herz und Mund,
Die so gern den Sternen klagen:
Leise doch im Herzensgrund
Bleibt das linde Wellenschlagen.

40. Sehnsucht

Es schienen so golden die Sterne,
Am Fenster ich einsam stand
Und hörte aus weiter Ferne
Ein Posthorn im stillen Land.
Das Herz mir im Leib entbrennte,
Da hab' ich mir heimlich gedacht:
Ach, wer da mitreisen könnte
In der prächtigen Sommernacht!

Zwei junge Gesellen gingen
Vorüber am Bergeshang,
Ich hörte im Wandern sie singen
Die stille Gegend entlang:

Von schwindelnden Felsenschlüften,
Wo die Wälder rauschen so sacht,
Von Quellen, die von den Klüften   15
Sich stürzen in die Waldesnacht.

Sie sangen von Marmorbildern,
Von Gärten, die überm Gestein
In dämmernden Lauben verwildern,
Palästen im Mondenschein,   20
Wo die Mädchen am Fenster lauschen,
Wann der Lauten Klang erwacht,
Und die Brunnen verschlafen rauschen
In der prächtigen Sommernacht.

41. Das zerbrochene Ringlein

In einem kühlen Grunde
Da geht ein Mühlenrad,
Mein' Liebste ist verschwunden,
Die dort gewohnet hat.

Sie hat mir Treu' versprochen,   5
Gab mir ein'n Ring dabei,
Sie hat die Treu' gebrochen,
Mein Ringlein sprang entzwei.

Ich möcht' als Spielmann reisen
Weit in die Welt hinaus,   10
Und singen meine Weisen,
Und gehn von Haus zu Haus.

Ich möcht' als Reiter fliegen
Wohl in die blut'ge Schlacht,
15   Um stille Feuer liegen
Im Feld bei dunkler Nacht.

Hör' ich das Mühlrad gehen:
Ich weiß nicht, was ich will —
Ich möcht' am liebsten sterben,
20   Da wär's auf einmal still.

42. Frühe

Im Osten graut's, der Nebel fällt,
Wer weiß, wie bald sich's rühret!
Doch schwer im Schlaf noch ruht die Welt,
Von allem nichts verspüret.

5   Nur eine frühe Lerche steigt,
Es hat ihr was geträumet
Vom Lichte, wenn noch alles schweigt,
Das kaum die Höhen säumet.

43. Nachts

Ich wandre durch die stille Nacht,
Da schleicht der Mond so heimlich sacht
Oft aus der dunklen Wolkenhülle,
Und hin und her im Tal
5   Erwacht die Nachtigall,
Dann wieder alles grau und stille.

O wunderbarer Nachtgesang:
Von fern im Land der Ströme Gang,
Leis Schauern in den dunklen Bäumen —
Wirrst die Gedanken mir,   10
Mein irres Singen hier
Ist wie ein Rufen nur aus Träumen.

44. Mondnacht

Es war, als hätt' der Himmel
Die Erde still geküßt,
Daß sie im Blütenschimmer
Von ihm nun träumen müßt'.

Die Luft ging durch die Felder,   5
Die Ähren wogten sacht,
Es rauschten leis die Wälder,
So sternklar war die Nacht.

Und meine Seele spannte
Weit ihre Flügel aus,   10
Flog durch die stillen Lande,
Als flöge sie nach Haus.

Friedrich Rückert

45. Aus der Jugendzeit

Aus der Jugendzeit, aus der Jugendzeit
Klingt ein Lied mir immerdar;
O wie liegt so weit, o wie liegt so weit,
Was mein einst war!

5   Was die Schwalbe sang, was die Schwalbe sang,
Die den Herbst und Frühling bringt;
Ob das Dorf entlang, ob das Dorf entlang
Das jetzt noch klingt?

   „Als ich Abschied nahm, als ich Abschied nahm,
10   Waren Kisten und Kasten schwer;
Als ich wieder kam, als ich wieder kam,
War alles leer."

   O du Kindermund, o du Kindermund,
Unbewußter Weisheit froh,
15   Vogelsprachekund, vogelsprachekund
Wie Salomo!

   O du Heimatflur, o du Heimatflur,
Laß zu deinem heil'gen Raum
Mich noch einmal nur, mich noch einmal nur
20   Entfliehn im Traum!

48

Als ich Abschied nahm, als ich Abschied nahm,
War die Welt mir voll so sehr;
Als ich wieder kam, als ich wieder kam,
War alles leer.

Wohl die Schwalbe kehrt, wohl die Schwalbe kehrt, 25
Und der leere Kasten schwoll,
Ist das Herz geleert, ist das Herz geleert,
Wird's nie mehr voll.

Keine Schwalbe bringt, keine Schwalbe bringt,
Dir zurück, wonach du weinst; 30
Doch die Schwalbe singt, doch die Schwalbe singt
Im Dorf wie einst:

„Als ich Abschied nahm, als ich Abschied nahm,
Waren Kisten und Kasten schwer;
Als ich wieder kam, als ich wieder kam, 35
War alles leer."

Heinrich Heine

46. Die Grenadiere

Nach Frankreich zogen zwei Grenadier',
Die waren in Rußland gefangen.
Und als sie kamen ins deutsche Quartier,
Sie ließen die Köpfe hangen.

5 Da hörten sie beide die traurige Mär':
Daß Frankreich verloren gegangen,
Besiegt und zerschlagen das große Heer, —
Und der Kaiser, der Kaiser gefangen.

Da weinten zusammen die Grenadier'
10 Wohl ob der kläglichen Kunde.
Der eine sprach: Wie weh wird mir,
Wie brennt meine alte Wunde!

Der andre sprach: Das Lied ist aus,
Auch ich möcht' mit dir sterben,
15 Doch hab' ich Weib und Kind zu Haus,
Die ohne mich verderben.

Was schert mich Weib, was schert mich Kind!
Ich trage weit beßres Verlangen;
Laß sie betteln gehn, wenn sie hungrig sind, —
20 Mein Kaiser, mein Kaiser gefangen!

Gewähr mir, Bruder, eine Bitt':
Wenn ich jetzt sterben werde,
So nimm meine Leiche nach Frankreich mit,
Begrab mich in Frankreichs Erde.

Das Ehrenkreuz am roten Band   25
Sollst du aufs Herz mir legen;
Die Flinte gib mir in die Hand,
Und gürt mir um den Degen.

So will ich liegen und horchen still,
Wie eine Schildwach', im Grabe,   30
Bis einst ich höre Kanonengebrüll
Und wiehernder Rosse Getrabe.

Dann reitet mein Kaiser wohl über mein Grab,
Viel Schwerter klirren und blitzen;
Dann steig' ich gewaffnet hervor aus dem Grab, — 35
Den Kaiser, den Kaiser zu schützen!

47.

In mein gar zu dunkles Leben
Strahlte einst ein süßes Bild;
Nun das süße Bild erblichen,
Bin ich gänzlich nachtumhüllt.

Wenn die Kinder sind im Dunkeln,   5
Wird beklommen ihr Gemüt,
Und um ihre Angst zu bannen,
Singen sie ein lautes Lied.

10

Ich, ein tolles Kind, ich singe
Jetzo in der Dunkelheit;
Klingt das Lied auch nicht ergötzlich,
Hat's mich doch von Angst befreit.

48.

Ich weiß nicht, was soll es bedeuten,
Daß ich so traurig bin;
Ein Märchen aus alten Zeiten,
Das kommt mir nicht aus dem Sinn.

5

Die Luft ist kühl und es dunkelt,
Und ruhig fließt der Rhein;
Der Gipfel des Berges funkelt
Im Abendsonnenschein.

Die schönste Jungfrau sitzet
Dort oben wunderbar,
Ihr goldnes Geschmeide blitzet,
Sie kämmt ihr goldenes Haar.

10

Sie kämmt es mit goldenem Kamme,
Und singt ein Lied dabei;
Das hat eine wundersame,
Gewaltige Melodei.

15

Den Schiffer im kleinen Schiffe
Ergreift es mit wildem Weh;
Er schaut nicht die Felsenriffe,
Er schaut nur hinauf in die Höh'.

20

Ich glaube, die Wellen verschlingen
Am Ende Schiffer und Kahn;
Und das hat mit ihrem Singen
Die Lorelei getan.

49.

Du bist wie eine Blume
So hold und schön und rein;
Ich schau' dich an, und Wehmut
Schleicht mir ins Herz hinein.

Mir ist, als ob ich die Hände   5
Aufs Haupt dir legen sollt',
Betend, daß Gott dich erhalte
So rein und schön und hold.

50.

Auf Flügeln des Gesanges,
Herzliebchen, trag' ich dich fort,
Fort nach den Fluren des Ganges,
Dort weiß ich den schönsten Ort.

Dort liegt ein rotblühender Garten   5
Im stillen Mondenschein;
Die Lotosblumen erwarten
Ihr trautes Schwesterlein.

Die Veilchen kichern und kosen,
Und schaun nach den Sternen empor;   10

Heimlich erzählen die Rosen
Sich duftende Märchen ins Ohr.

Es hüpfen herbei und lauschen
Die frommen, klugen Gazell'n;
15   Und in der Ferne rauschen
Des heiligen Stromes Well'n.

Dort wollen wir niedersinken
Unter dem Palmenbaum,
Und Liebe und Ruhe trinken
20   Und träumen seligen Traum.

51.

Die Lotosblume ängstigt
Sich vor der Sonne Pracht,
Und mit gesenktem Haupte
Erwartet sie träumend die Nacht.

5   Der Mond, der ist ihr Buhle,
Er weckt sie mit seinem Licht,
Und ihm entschleiert sie freundlich
Ihr frommes Blumengesicht.

Sie blüht und glüht und leuchtet,
10   Und starret stumm in die Höh';
Sie duftet und weinet und zittert
Vor Liebe und Liebesweh.

52.

Ein Fichtenbaum steht einsam
Im Norden auf kahler Höh'.
Ihn schläfert; mit weißer Decke
Umhüllen ihn Eis und Schnee.

Er träumt von einer Palme,   5
Die fern im Morgenland
Einsam und schweigend trauert
Auf brennender Felsenwand.

53.

Mein Liebchen, wir saßen beisammen,
Traulich im leichten Kahn.
Die Nacht war still, und wir schwammen
Auf weiter Wasserbahn.

Die Geisterinsel, die schöne,   5
Lag dämmrig im Mondenglanz;
Dort klangen liebe Töne,
Und wogte der Nebeltanz.

Dort klang es lieb und lieber,
Und wogt' es hin und her;   10
Wir aber schwammen vorüber
Trostlos auf weitem Meer.

54.

Ein Jüngling liebt ein Mädchen,
Die hat einen andern erwählt;
Der andre liebt eine andre,
Und hat sich mit dieser vermählt.

5   Das Mädchen heiratet aus Ärger
Den ersten besten Mann,
Der ihr in den Weg gelaufen;
Der Jüngling ist übel dran.

Es ist eine alte Geschichte,
10   Doch bleibt sie immer neu;
Und wem sie just passieret,
Dem bricht das Herz entzwei.

55.

Dämmernd liegt der Sommerabend
Über Wald und grünen Wiesen;
Goldner Mond im blauen Himmel
Strahlt herunter, duftig labend.

5   An dem Bache zirpt die Grille,
Und es regt sich in dem Wasser,
Und der Wandrer hört ein Plätschern
Und ein Atmen in der Stille.

Dorten, an dem Bach alleine,
10   Badet sich die schöne Elfe;
Arm und Nacken, weiß und lieblich,
Schimmern in dem Mondenscheine.

56.

Es fällt ein Stern herunter
Aus seiner funkelnden Höh'!
Das ist der Stern der Liebe,
Den ich dort fallen seh'.

Es fallen vom Apfelbaume   5
Der Blüten und Blätter viel.
Es kommen die neckenden Lüfte
Und treiben damit ihr Spiel.

Es singt der Schwan im Weiher
Und rudert auf und ab,   10
Und immer leiser singend
Taucht er ins Flutengrab.

Es ist so still und dunkel!
Verweht ist Blatt und Blüt',
Der Stern ist knisternd zerstoben,   15
Verklungen das Schwanenlied.

57.

Der Tod, das ist die kühle Nacht,
Das Leben ist der schwüle Tag.
Es dunkelt schon, mich schläfert,
Der Tag hat mich müd' gemacht.

Über mein Bett erhebt sich ein Baum   5
Drin singt die junge Nachtigall;
Sie singt von lauter Liebe,
Ich hör' es sogar im Traum.

58.

„Sag, wo ist dein schönes Liebchen,
Das du einst so schön besungen,
Als die zaubermächt'gen Flammen
Wunderbar dein Herz durchdrungen?"

5   Jene Flammen sind erloschen,
Und mein Herz ist kalt und trübe,
Und dies Büchlein ist die Urne
Mit der Asche meiner Liebe.

59. Frieden

Hoch am Himmel stand die Sonne
Von weißen Wolken umwogt,
Das Meer war still,
Und sinnend lag ich am Steuer des Schiffes,
5   Träumerisch sinnend — und, halb im Wachen
Und halb im Schlummer, schaute ich Christus,
Den Heiland der Welt.
Im wallend weißen Gewande
Wandelt' er riesengroß
10   Über Land und Meer;
Es ragte sein Haupt in den Himmel,
Die Hände streckte er segnend
Über Land und Meer;
Und als ein Herz in der Brust
15   Trug er die Sonne,

Die rote, flammende Sonne;
Und das rote, flammende Sonnenherz
Goß seine Gnadenstrahlen
Und sein holdes, liebseliges Licht,
Erleuchtend und wärmend   20
Über Land und Meer.

Glockenklänge zogen feierlich
Hin und her, zogen wie Schwäne,
An Rosenbändern, das gleitende Schiff,
Und zogen es spielend ans grüne Ufer,   25
Wo Menschen wohnen, in hochgetürmter,
Ragender Stadt.

O Friedenswunder! Wie still die Stadt!
Es ruhte das dumpfe Geräusch
Der schwatzenden, schwülen Gewerbe,   30
Und durch die reinen, hallenden Straßen
Wandelten Menschen, weißgekleidete,
Palmzweig=tragende,
Und wo sich zwei begegneten,
Sah'n sie sich an, verständnisinnig,   35
Und schauernd in Liebe und süßer Entsagung
Küßten sie sich auf die Stirne,
Und schauten hinauf
Nach des Heilands Sonnenherzen,
Das freudig versöhnend sein rotes Blut   40
Hinunterstrahlte,
Und dreimalselig sprachen sie:
„Gelobt sei Jesus Christ!"

60

Leise zieht durch mein Gemüt
Liebliches Geläute.
Klinge, kleines Frühlingslied,
Kling hinaus ins Weite.

5   Kling hinaus, bis an das Haus,
Wo die Blumen sprießen.
Wenn du eine Rose schaust,
Sag, ich laß' sie grüßen.

61.

Es war ein alter König,
Sein Herz war schwer, sein Haupt war grau;
Der arme alte König,
Er nahm eine junge Frau.

5   Es war ein schöner Page,
Blond war sein Haupt, leicht war sein Sinn;
Er trug die seidne Schleppe
Der jungen Königin.

Kennst du das alte Liedchen?
10   Es klingt so süß, es klingt so trüb'!
Sie mußten beide sterben,
Sie hatten sich viel zu lieb.

62.

Es ziehen die brausenden Wellen
Wohl nach dem Strand;
Sie schwellen und zerschellen
Wohl auf dem Sand.

Sie kommen groß und kräftig   5
Ohn' Unterlaß;
Sie werden endlich heftig —
Was hilft uns das?

63.

Es ragt ins Meer der Runenstein,
Da sitz' ich mit meinen Träumen.
Es pfeift der Wind, die Möwen schrein,
Die Wellen, die wandern und schäumen.

Ich habe geliebt manch schönes Kind   5
Und manchen guten Gesellen —
Wo sind sie hin? Es pfeift der Wind,
Es schäumen und wandern die Wellen.

64. In der Fremde

Ich hatte einst ein schönes Vaterland.
Der Eichenbaum
Wuchs dort so hoch, die Veilchen nickten sanft.
Es war ein Traum.

5   Das küßte mich auf deutsch und sprach auf deutsch
(Man glaubt es kaum,
Wie gut es klang) das Wort: „Ich liebe dich!"
Es war ein Traum.

65. Der Asra

Täglich ging die wunderschöne
Sultanstochter auf und nieder
Um die Abendzeit am Springbrunn,
Wo die weißen Wasser plätschern.

5.   Täglich stand der junge Sklave
Um die Abendzeit am Springbrunn,
Wo die weißen Wasser plätschern;
Täglich ward er bleich und bleicher.

Eines Abends trat die Fürstin
10   Auf ihn zu mit raschen Worten:
„Deinen Namen will ich wissen,
Deine Heimat, deine Sippschaft!"

Und der Sklave sprach: „Ich heiße
Mohamet, ich bin aus Yemmen,
15   Und mein Stamm sind jene Asra,
Welche sterben, wenn sie lieben."

August, Graf von Platen

66. Das Grab im Busento

Nächtlich am Busento lispeln bei Cosenza dumpfe Lieder;
Aus den Wassern schallt es Antwort, und in Wirbeln klingt
es wieder!

Und den Fluß hinauf, hinunter ziehn die Schatten tapfrer
Goten,
Die den Alarich beweinen, ihres Volkes besten Toten.

Allzufrüh und fern der Heimat mußten hier sie ihn be= 5
graben,
Während noch die Jugendlocken seine Schulter blond um=
gaben.

Und am Ufer des Busento reihten sie sich um die Wette,
Um die Strömung abzuleiten, gruben sie ein frisches Bette.

In der wogenleeren Höhlung wühlten sie empor die Erde,
Senkten tief hinein den Leichnam, mit der Rüstung, auf 10
dem Pferde.

Deckten dann mit Erde wieder ihn und seine stolze Habe,
Daß die hohen Stromgewächse wüchsen aus dem Helden=
grabe.

Abgelenkt zum zweiten Male, ward der Fluß herbeigezogen:
Mächtig in ihr altes Bette schäumten die Busentowogen.

15 Und es sang ein Chor von Männern: „Schlaf in deinen
    Heldenehren!
Keines Römers schnöde Habsucht soll dir je dein Grab
    versehren!"

Sangen's, und die Lobgesänge tönten fort im Gotenheere;
Wälze sie, Busentowelle, wälze sie von Meer zu Meere!

67.

Im Wasser wogt die Lilie, die blanke, hin und her,
Doch irrst du, Freund, sobald du sagst, sie schwanke hin und
    her:
Es wurzelt ja so fest ihr Fuß im tiefen Meeresgrund,
Ihr Haupt nur wiegt ein lieblicher Gedanke hin und her!

68.

Wie rafft' ich mich auf in der Nacht, in der Nacht,
Und fühlte mich fürder gezogen,
Die Gassen verließ ich, vom Wächter bewacht,
    Durchwandelte sacht
5   In der Nacht, in der Nacht,
Das Tor mit dem gotischen Bogen.

Der Mühlbach rauschte durch felsigen Schacht,
Ich lehnte mich über die Brücke,
Tief unter mir nahm ich der Wogen in acht,
10   Die wallten so sacht
    In der Nacht, in der Nacht,
Doch wallte nicht eine zurücke.

Es drehte sich oben, unzählig entfacht,
Melodischer Wandel der Sterne,
Mit ihnen der Mond in beruhigter Pracht, 15
   Sie funkelten sacht
   In der Nacht, in der Nacht,
Durch täuschend entlegene Ferne.

Ich blickte hinauf in der Nacht, in der Nacht,
Ich blickte hinunter aufs neue: 20
O wehe, wie hast du die Tage verbracht,
   Nun stille du sacht
   In der Nacht, in der Nacht,
Im pochenden Herzen die Reue!

69.

Ich möchte, wann ich sterbe, wie die lichten
Gestirne schnell und unbewußt erbleichen,
Erliegen möcht' ich einst des Todes Streichen,
Wie Sagen uns vom Pindaros berichten.

Ich will ja nicht im Leben oder Dichten 5
Den großen Unerreichlichen erreichen,
Ich möcht', o Freund, ihm nur im Tode gleichen;
Doch höre nun die schönste der Geschichten!

Er saß im Schauspiel, vom Gesang beweget,
Und hatte, der ermüdet war, die Wangen 10
Auf seines Lieblings schönes Knie geleget:

Als nun der Chöre Melodien verklangen,
Will wecken ihn, der ihn so sanft geheget,
Doch zu den Göttern war er heimgegangen.

Nikolaus Lenau

70. Bitte

Weil' auf mir, du dunkles Auge,
Übe deine ganze Macht,
Ernste, milde, träumerische,
Unergründlich süße Nacht!

5 Nimm mit deinem Zauberdunkel
Diese Welt von hinnen mir,
Daß du über meinem Leben
Einsam schwebest für und für.

71. Schilflied

Auf dem Teich, dem regungslosen,
Weilt des Mondes holder Glanz,
Flechtend seine bleichen Rosen
In des Schilfes grünen Kranz.

5 Hirsche wandeln dort am Hügel,
Blicken in die Nacht empor;
Manchmal regt sich das Geflügel
Träumerisch im tiefen Rohr.

Weinend muß mein Blick sich senken;
10 Durch die tiefste Seele geht
Mir ein süßes Deingedenken
Wie ein stilles Nachtgebet!

72. Der Eichwald

Ich trat in einen heilig düstern
Eichwald, da hört' ich leis' und lind
Ein Bächlein unter Blumen flüstern,
Wie das Gebet von einem Kind;

Und mich ergriff ein süßes Grauen,　　　　5
Es rauscht' der Wald geheimnisvoll,
Als möcht' er mir was anvertrauen,
Das noch mein Herz nicht wissen soll;

Als möcht' er heimlich mir entdecken,
Was Gottes Liebe sinnt und will:　　　　10
Doch schien er plötzlich zu erschrecken
Vor Gottes Näh' — und wurde still.

73. Der Postillion

Lieblich war die Maiennacht,
Silberwölklein flogen,
Ob der holden Frühlingspracht
Freudig hingezogen.

Schlummernd lagen Wies' und Hain,　　　　5
Jeder Pfad verlassen;
Niemand als der Mondenschein
Wachte auf der Straßen.

Leise nur das Lüftchen sprach,
Und es zog gelinder
Durch das stille Schlafgemach
All der Frühlingskinder.

Heimlich nur das Bächlein schlich,
Denn der Blüten Träume
Dufteten gar wonniglich
Durch die stillen Räume.

Rauher war mein Postillion,
Ließ die Geißel knallen,
Über Berg und Tal davon
Frisch sein Horn erschallen.

Und von flinken Rossen vier
Scholl der Hufe Schlagen,
Die durchs blühende Revier
Trabten mit Behagen.

Wald und Flur im schnellen Zug
Kaum gegrüßt — gemieden;
Und vorbei, wie Traumesflug,
Schwand der Dörfer Frieden.

Mitten in dem Maienglück
Lag ein Kirchhof innen,
Der den raschen Wanderblick
Hielt zu ernstem Sinnen.

Hingelehnt an Bergesrand
War die bleiche Mauer,
Und das Kreuzbild Gottes stand
Hoch, in stummer Trauer.

Schwager ritt auf seiner Bahn
Stiller jetzt und trüber;
Und die Rosse hielt er an,
Sah zum Kreuz hinüber: 40

„Halten muß hier Roß und Rad,
Mag's Euch nicht gefährden;
Drüben liegt mein Kamerad
In der kühlen Erden!

Ein gar herzlieber Gesell!   45
Herr, 's ist ewig schade!
Keiner blies das Horn so hell,
Wie mein Kamerade!

Hier ich immer halten muß,
Dem dort unterm Rasen   50
Zum getreuen Brudergruß
Sein Leiblied zu blasen!"

Und dem Kirchhof sandt' er zu
Frohe Wandersänge,
Daß es in die Grabesruh'   55
Seinem Bruder dränge.

Und des Hornes heller Ton
Klang vom Berge wieder,
Ob der tote Postillion
Stimmt' in seine Lieder. —   60

Weiter ging's durch Feld und Hag
Mit verhängtem Zügel;
Lang mir noch im Ohre lag
Jener Klang vom Hügel.

74. Die Drei

Drei Reiter nach verlorner Schlacht,
Wie reiten sie so sacht, so sacht!

Aus tiefen Wunden quillt das Blut,
Es spürt das Roß die warme Flut.

5   Vom Sattel tropft das Blut, vom Zaum,
Und spült hinunter Staub und Schaum.

Die Rosse schreiten sanft und weich,
Sonst flöß' das Blut zu rasch, zu reich.

Die Reiter reiten dicht gesellt,
10   Und einer sich am andern hält.

Sie sehn sich traurig ins Gesicht,
Und einer um den andern spricht:

„Mir blüht daheim die schönste Maid,
Drum tut mein früher Tod mir leid."

15   „Hab' Haus und Hof und grünen Wald,
Und sterben muß ich hier so bald!"

„Den Blick hab' ich in Gottes Welt,
Sonst nichts, doch schwer mir's Sterben fällt."

Und lauernd auf den Todesritt
20   Ziehn durch die Luft drei Geier mit.

Sie teilen kreischend unter sich:
„Den speisest du, den du, den ich".

75. Der offene Schrank

Mein liebes Mütterlein war verreist,
Und kehrte nicht heim, und lag in der Grube;
Da war ich allein und recht verwaist,
Und traurig trat ich in ihre Stube.

Ihr Schrank stand offen, ich fand ihn noch heut',   5
Wie sie, abreisend, ihn eilig gelassen,
Wie alles man durcheinander streut,
Wenn vor der Tür die Pferde schon passen.

Ein aufgeschlagnes Gebetbuch lag
Bei mancher Rechnung, von ihr geschrieben;   10
Von ihrem Frühstück am Scheidetag
War noch ein Stücklein Kuchen geblieben.

Ich las das aufgeschlagne Gebet,
Es war: wie eine Mutter um Segen
Für ihre Kinder zum Himmel fleht;   15
Mir pochte das Herz in bangen Schlägen.

Ich las ihre Schrift, und ich verbiß
Nicht länger meine gerechten Schmerzen,
Ich las die Zahlen, und ich zerriß
Die Freudenrechnung in meinem Herzen.   20

Zusammen sucht' ich den Speiserest,
Das kleinste Krümlein, den letzten Splitter,
Und hätt' es mir auch den Hals gepreßt,
Ich aß vom Kuchen und weinte bitter.

76. Auf eine holländische Landschaft

Müde schleichen hier die Bäche,
Nicht ein Lüftchen hörst du wallen,
Die entfärbten Blätter fallen
Still zu Grund', vor Altersschwäche.

5   Krähen, kaum die Schwingen regend,
Streichen langsam; dort am Hügel
Läßt die Windmühl' ruhn die Flügel;
Ach, wie schläfrig ist die Gegend!

Lenz und Sommer sind verflogen;
10 Dort das Hüttlein, ob es trutze,
Blickt nicht aus, die Strohkapuze
Tief ins Aug' herabgezogen.

Schlummernd, oder träge sinnend,
Ruht der Hirt bei seinen Schafen,
15 Die Natur, Herbstnebel spinnend,
Scheint am Rocken eingeschlafen.

77. Stimme des Regens

Die Lüfte rasten auf der weiten Heide,
Die Disteln sind so regungslos zu schauen,
So starr, als wären sie aus Stein gehauen,
Bis sie der Wandrer streift mit seinem Kleide.

5   Und Erd' und Himmel haben keine Scheide,
In eins gefallen sind die nebelgrauen,

Zwei Freunden gleich, die sich ihr Leid vertrauen,
Und mein und dein vergessen traurig beide.

Nun plötzlich wankt die Distel hin und wieder,
Und heftig rauschend bricht der Regen nieder,   10
Wie laute Antwort auf ein stummes Fragen.

Der Wandrer hört den Regen niederbrausen,
Er hört die windgepeitschte Distel sausen,
Und eine Wehmut fühlt er, nicht zu sagen.

78. Herbst

Rings ein Verstummen, ein Entfärben:
Wie sanft den Wald die Lüfte streicheln,
Sein welkes Laub ihm abzuschmeicheln;
Ich liebe dieses milde Sterben.

Von hinnen geht die stille Reise,   5
Die Zeit der Liebe ist verklungen,
Die Vögel haben ausgesungen,
Und dürre Blätter sinken leise.

Die Vögel zogen nach dem Süden,
Aus dem Verfall des Laubes tauchen   10
Die Nester, die nicht Schutz mehr brauchen,
Die Blätter fallen stets, die müden.

In dieses Waldes leisem Rauschen
Ist mir, als hör' ich Kunde wehen,
Daß alles Sterben und Vergehen   15
Nur heimlich still vergnügtes Tauschen.

Eduard Mörike

79. Um Mitternacht

Gelassen stieg die Nacht ans Land,
Lehnt träumend an der Berge Wand;
Ihr Auge sieht die goldne Wage nun
Der Zeit in gleichen Schalen stille ruhn.
5   Und kecker rauschen die Quellen hervor,
    Sie singen der Mutter, der Nacht, ins Ohr
      Vom Tage,
Vom heute gewesenen Tage.

Das uralt alte Schlummerlied —
10   Sie achtet's nicht, sie ist es müd';
Ihr klingt des Himmels Bläue süßer noch,
Der flücht'gen Stunden gleichgeschwung'nes Joch.
    Doch immer behalten die Quellen das Wort,
    Es singen die Wasser im Schlafe noch fort
15   Vom Tage,
Vom heute gewesenen Tage.

80. Septembermorgen

Im Nebel ruhet noch die Welt,
Noch träumen Wald und Wiesen:
Bald siehst du, wenn der Schleier fällt,
Den blauen Himmel unverstellt,
5   Herbstkräftig die gedämpfte Welt
In warmem Golde fließen.

81. Er ist's

Frühling läßt sein blaues Band
Wieder flattern durch die Lüfte;
Süße, wohlbekannte Düfte
Streifen ahnungsvoll das Land.
Veilchen träumen schon,   5
Wollen balde kommen. —
Horch, von fern ein leiser Harfenton!
    Frühling, ja du bist's!
Dich hab' ich vernommen!

82. In der Frühe

Kein Schlaf noch kühlt das Auge mir,
Dort gehet schon der Tag herfür
An meinem Kammerfenster.
Es wühlet mein verstörter Sinn
Noch zwischen Zweifeln her und hin   5
Und schaffet Nachtgespenster. —
Ängste, quäle
Dich nicht länger, meine Seele!
Freu dich! schon sind da und dorten
Morgenglocken wach geworden.   10

83. Der Feuerreiter

Sehet ihr am Fensterlein
Dort die rote Mütze wieder?
Nicht geheuer muß es sein,
Denn er geht schon auf und nieder.

5
Und auf einmal welch Gewühle
Bei der Brücke, nach dem Feld!
Horch! das Feuerglöcklein gellt:
    Hinterm Berg,
    Hinterm Berg
10
Brennt es in der Mühle.

Schaut! da sprengt er wütend schier
Durch das Tor, der Feuerreiter,
Auf dem rippendürren Tier,
Als auf einer Feuerleiter.
15
Querfeldein! Durch Qualm und Schwüle
Rennt er schon und ist am Ort!
Drüben schallt es fort und fort:
    Hinterm Berg,
    Hinterm Berg
20
Brennt es in der Mühle.

Der so oft den roten Hahn
Meilenweit von fern gerochen,
Mit des heil'gen Kreuzes Span
Freventlich die Glut besprochen —
25
Weh! dir grinst vom Dachgestühle
Dort der Feind im Höllenschein.
Gnade Gott der Seele dein!
    Hinterm Berg,
    Hinterm Berg
30
Rast er in der Mühle.

Keine Stunde hielt es an,
Bis die Mühle borst in Trümmer;
Doch den kecken Reitersmann
Sah man von der Stunde nimmer.

Volk und Wagen im Gewühle   35
Kehren heim von all dem Graus;
Auch das Glöcklein klinget aus:
    Hinterm Berg,
    Hinterm Berg
Brennt's —   40

Nach der Zeit ein Müller fand
Ein Gerippe samt der Mützen
Aufrecht an der Kellerwand
Auf der beinern Mähre sitzen.
Feuerreiter, wie so kühle   45
Reitest du in deinem Grab!
Husch! da fällt's in Asche ab.
    Ruhe wohl,
    Ruhe wohl
Drunten in der Mühle!   50

84. Das verlassene Mägdlein

Früh, wann die Hähne krähn,
Eh' die Sternlein verschwinden,
Muß ich am Herde stehn,
Muß Feuer zünden.

Schön ist der Flammen Schein,   5
Es springen die Funken;
Ich schaue so drein,
In Leid versunken.

Plötzlich da kommt es mir,
10 Treuloser Knabe,
Daß ich die Nacht von dir
Geträumet habe.

Träne auf Träne dann
Stürzet hernieder:
15 So kommt der Tag heran —
O ging' er wieder!

85. Lebewohl

„Lebe wohl!" — Du fühlest nicht,
Was es heißt, dies Wort der Schmerzen;
Mit getrostem Angesicht
Sagtest du's und leichtem Herzen.

5 Lebe wohl! — Ach, tausendmal
Hab' ich mir es vorgesprochen,
Und in nimmersatter Qual
Mir das Herz damit gebrochen!

86 Schön=Rohtraut

Wie heißt König Ringangs Töchterlein?
    Rohtraut, Schön=Rohtraut.
Was tut sie denn den ganzen Tag,
Da sie wohl nicht spinnen und nähen mag?
5   Tut fischen und jagen.

O daß ich doch ihr Jäger wär'!
Fischen und Jagen freute mich sehr. —
    Schweig stille, mein Herze!

Und über eine kleine Weil',
    Rohtraut, Schön=Rohtraut,   10
So dient der Knab' auf Ringangs Schloß
In Jägertracht und hat ein Roß,
    Mit Rohtraut zu jagen.
O daß ich doch ein Königssohn wär'!
Rohtraut, Schön=Rohtraut lieb' ich so sehr. —   15
    Schweig stille, mein Herze!

Einstmals sie ruhten am Eichenbaum,
    Da lacht Schön=Rohtraut:
„Was siehst mich an so wunniglich?
Wenn du das Herz hast, küsse mich!"   20
    Ach, erschrak der Knabe!
Doch denket er: Mir ist's vergunnt,
Und küsset Schön=Rohtraut auf den Mund. —
    Schweig stille, mein Herze!

Darauf sie ritten schweigend heim,   25
    Rohtraut, Schön=Rohtraut;
Es jauchzt der Knab' in seinem Sinn:
Und würdst du heute Kaiserin,
    Mich sollt's nicht kränken!
Ihr tausend Blätter im Walde, wißt!   30
Ich hab' Schön=Rohtrauts Mund geküßt —
    Schweig stille, mein Herze!

87. Auf eine Lampe

Noch unverrückt, o schöne Lampe, schmückest du,
An leichten Ketten zierlich aufgehangen hier,
Die Decke des nun fast vergeßnen Lustgemachs.
Auf deiner weißen Marmorschale, deren Rand
5　Der Efeukranz von goldengrünem Erz umflicht,
Schlingt fröhlich eine Kinderschar den Ringelreihn.
Wie reizend alles! lachend und ein sanfter Geist
Des Ernstes doch ergossen um die ganze Form:
Ein Kunstgebild der echten Art. Wer achtet sein?
10　Was aber schön ist, selig scheint es in ihm selbst.

88. Gebet

Herr, schicke, was du willt,
Ein Liebes oder Leides!
Ich bin vergnügt, daß beides
Aus deinen Händen quillt.

5　Wollest mit Freuden
Und wollest mit Leiden
Mich nicht überschütten!
Doch in der Mitten
Liegt holdes Bescheiden.

89. Denk' es, o Seele

Ein Tännlein grünet wo,
Wer weiß? im Walde,

Ein Rosenstrauch, wer sagt,
In welchem Garten?
Sie sind erlesen schon —   5
Denk' es, o Seele! —
Auf deinem Grab zu wurzeln
Und zu wachsen.

Zwei schwarze Rößlein weiden
Auf der Wiese,   10
Sie kehren heim zur Stadt
In muntern Sprüngen.
Sie werden schrittweis gehn
Mit deiner Leiche,
Vielleicht, vielleicht noch eh'   15
An ihren Hufen
Das Eisen los wird,
Das ich blitzen sehe.

Friedrich Hebbel

90. Nachtlied

Quellende, schwellende Nacht,
  Voll von Lichtern und Sternen,
  In den ewigen Fernen,
Sage, was ist da erwacht?

5   Herz in der Brust wird beengt,
  Steigendes, neigendes Leben,
  Riesenhaft fühle ich's weben,
Welches das meine verdrängt.

Schlaf, da nahst du dich leis,
10   Wie dem Kinde die Amme,
  Und um die dürftige Flamme
Ziehst du den schützenden Kreis.

91. Das Kind

Die Mutter lag im Totenschrein,
  Zum letztenmal geschmückt;
Da spielt das kleine Kind herein,
  Das staunend sie erblickt.

Die Blumenkron' im blonden Haar   5
    Gefällt ihm gar zu sehr,
Die Busenblumen, bunt und klar,
    Zum Strauß gereiht, noch mehr.

Und sanft und schmeichelnd ruft es aus:
    „Du liebe Mutter, gib   10
Mir eine Blum' aus deinem Strauß,
    Ich hab' dich auch so lieb."

Und als die Mutter es nicht tut,
    Da denkt das Kind für sich:
„Sie schläft, doch wenn sie ausgeruht,   15
    So tut sie's sicherlich."

Schleicht fort, so leis' es immer kann,
    Und schließt die Türe sacht
Und lauscht von Zeit zu Zeit daran,
    Ob Mutter noch nicht wacht.   20

92. Nachtgefühl

Wenn ich mich abends entkleide,
    Gemachsam, Stück für Stück,
So tragen die müden Gedanken
    Mich vorwärts oder zurück.

Ich denke der alten Tage,   5
    Da zog die Mutter mich aus;
Sie legte mich still in die Wiege,
    Die Winde brausten ums Haus.

Ich denke der letzten Stunde,
10   Da werden 's die Nachbarn tun;
Sie senken mich still in die Erde,
    Da werd' ich lange ruhn.

Schließt nun der Schlaf mein Auge,
    Wie träum' ich so oftmals das:
15   Es wäre eins von beidem,
    Nur wüßt' ich selber nicht, was.

93. Gebet

Die du, über die Sterne weg,
    Mit der geleerten Schale
Aufschwebst, um sie am ew'gen Born
    Eilig wieder zu füllen:
5   Einmal schwenke sie noch, o Glück,
    Einmal, lächelnde Göttin!
Sieh, ein einziger Tropfen hängt
    Noch verloren am Rande,
Und der einzige Tropfen genügt,
10   Eine himmlische Seele,
Die hier unten in Schmerz erstarrt,
    Wieder in Wonne zu lösen.
Ach! sie weint dir süßeren Dank,
    Als die anderen alle,
15   Die du glücklich und reich gemacht;
    Laß ihn fallen, den Tropfen!

94. Abendgefühl

Friedlich bekämpfen
   Nacht sich und Tag.
Wie das zu dämpfen,
   Wie das zu lösen vermag!

Der mich bedrückte,   5
   Schläfst du schon, Schmerz?
Was mich beglückte,
   Sage, was war 's doch, mein Herz?

Freude wie Kummer,
   Fühl' ich, zerrann,   10
Aber den Schlummer
   Führten sie leise heran.

Und im Entschweben,
   Immer empor,
Kommt mir das Leben   15
   Ganz wie ein Schlummerlied vor.

95. Ich und du

Wir träumten von einander
   Und sind davon erwacht,
Wir leben, um uns zu lieben,
   Und sinken zurück in die Nacht.

Du tratst aus meinem Traume,   5
   Aus deinem trat ich hervor,
Wir sterben, wenn sich eines
   Im andern ganz verlor.

Auf einer Lilie zittern
10   Zwei Tropfen, rein und rund,
Zerfließen in eins und rollen
     Hinab in des Kelches Grund.

96. Sommerbild

Ich sah des Sommers letzte Rose stehn,
     Sie war, als ob sie bluten könne, rot;
Da sprach ich schauernd im Vorübergehn:
     „So weit im Leben ist zu nah' am Tod."

5   Es regte sich kein Hauch am heißen Tag,
     Nur leise strich ein weißer Schmetterling;
Doch ob auch kaum die Luft sein Flügelschlag
     Bewegte, sie empfand es und verging.

97. Herbstbild

Dies ist ein Herbsttag, wie ich keinen sah!
     Die Luft ist still, als atmete man kaum,
Und dennoch fallen, raschelnd, fern und nah,
     Die schönsten Früchte ab von jedem Baum.

5   O stört sie nicht, die Feier der Natur!
     Dies ist die Lese, die sie selber hält,
Denn heute löst sich von den Zweigen nur,
     Was vor dem milden Strahl der Sonne fällt.

Gottfried Keller

98. An das Vaterland

O mein Heimatland! O mein Vaterland!
Wie so innig, feurig lieb' ich dich!
Schönste Ros', ob jede mir verblich,
Duftest noch an meinem öden Strand!

Als ich arm, doch froh, fremdes Land durchstrich,   5
Königsglanz mit deinen Bergen maß,
Thronenflitter bald ob dir vergaß,
Wie war da der Bettler stolz auf dich!

Als ich fern dir war, o Helvetia!
Faßte manchmal mich ein tiefes Leid;   10
Doch wie kehrte schnell es sich in Freud',
Wenn ich einen deiner Söhne sah!

O mein Schweizerland, all mein Gut und Hab!
Wann dereinst die letzte Stunde kommt,
Ob ich Schwacher dir auch nichts gefrommt,   15
Nicht versage mir ein stilles Grab!

Werf' ich von mir einst dies mein Staubgewand,
Beten will ich dann zu Gott dem Herrn:
„Lasse strahlen deinen schönsten Stern
Nieder auf mein irdisch Vaterland!"   20

99. Winternacht

Nicht ein Flügelschlag ging durch die Welt,
Still und blendend lag der weiße Schnee.
Nicht ein Wölklein hing am Sternenzelt,
Keine Welle schlug im starren See.

5   Aus der Tiefe stieg der Seebaum auf,
Bis sein Wipfel in dem Eis gefror;
An den Ästen klomm die Nix' herauf,
Schaute durch das grüne Eis empor.

Auf dem dünnen Glase stand ich da,
10   Das die schwarze Tiefe von mir schied;
Dicht ich unter meinen Füßen sah
Ihre weiße Schönheit, Glied um Glied.

Mit ersticktem Jammer tastet sie
An der harten Decke her und hin,
15   Ich vergess' das dunkle Antlitz nie,
Immer, immer liegt es mir im Sinn.

100. Abendlied

Augen, meine lieben Fensterlein,
Gebt mir schon so lange holden Schein,
Lasset freundlich Bild um Bild herein:
Einmal werdet ihr verdunkelt sein!

Fallen einst die müden Lider zu, 5
Löscht ihr aus, dann hat die Seele Ruh';
Tastend streift sie ab die Wanderschuh',
Legt sich auch in ihre finstre Truh'.

Noch zwei Fünklein sieht sie glimmend stehn
Wie zwei Sternlein, innerlich zu sehn, 10
Bis sie schwanken und dann auch vergehn,
Wie von eines Falters Flügelwehn.

Doch noch wandl' ich auf dem Abendfeld,
Nur dem sinkenden Gestirn gesellt;
Trinkt, o Augen, was die Wimper hält, 15
Von dem goldnen Überfluß der Welt!

101. Unter Sternen

Wende dich, du kleiner Stern,
Erde! wo ich lebe,
Daß mein Aug', der Sonne fern,
Sternenwärts sich hebe!

Heilig ist die Sternenzeit, 5
Öffnet alle Grüfte;
Strahlende Unsterblichkeit
Wandelt durch die Lüfte.

Mag die Sonne nun bislang
Andern Zonen scheinen, 10
Hier fühl' ich Zusammenhang
Mit dem All' und Einen!

Hohe Luft, im dunklen Tal,
Selber ungesehen,
15   Durch den majestät'schen Saal
Atmend mitzugehen!

Schwinge dich, o grünes Rund,
In die Morgenröte!
Scheidend rückwärts singt mein Mund
20   Jubelnde Gebete!

Theodor Storm

102. Oktoberlied

Der Nebel steigt, es fällt das Laub;
Schenk ein den Wein, den holden!
Wir wollen uns den grauen Tag
Vergolden, ja vergolden!

Und geht es draußen noch so toll,   5
Unchristlich oder christlich,
Ist doch die Welt, die schöne Welt,
So gänzlich unverwüstlich!

Und wimmert auch einmal das Herz, —
Stoß an und laß es klingen!   10
Wir wissen's doch, ein rechtes Herz
Ist gar nicht umzubringen.

Der Nebel steigt, es fällt das Laub;
Schenk ein den Wein, den holden!
Wir wollen uns den grauen Tag   15
Vergolden, ja vergolden!

Wohl ist es Herbst; doch warte nur,
Doch warte nur ein Weilchen!
Der Frühling kommt, der Himmel lacht,
Es steht die Welt in Veilchen.   20

Die blauen Tage brechen an,
Und ehe sie verfließen,
Wir wollen sie, mein wackrer Freund,
Genießen, ja genießen!

103. Weihnachtslied

Vom Himmel in die tiefsten Klüfte
Ein milder Stern herniederlacht;
Vom Tannenwalde steigen Düfte
Und hauchen durch die Winterlüfte,
5   Und kerzenhelle wird die Nacht.

Mir ist das Herz so froh erschrocken,
Das ist die liebe Weihnachtszeit!
Ich höre fernher Kirchenglocken
Mich lieblich heimatlich verlocken
10   In märchenstille Heimlichkeit.

Ein frommer Zauber hält mich wieder,
Anbetend, staunend muß ich stehn;
Es sinkt auf meine Augenlider
Ein goldner Kindertraum hernieder,
15   Ich fühl's: ein Wunder ist geschehn.

104. Sommermittag

Nun ist es still um Hof und Scheuer,
Und in der Mühle ruht der Stein;
Der Birnenbaum mit blanken Blättern
Steht regungslos im Sonnenschein.

Die Bienen summen so verschlafen; 5
Und in der offnen Bodenluk',
Benebelt von dem Duft des Heues,
Im grauen Röcklein nickt der Puk.

Der Müller schnarcht und das Gesinde,
Und nur die Tochter wacht im Haus; 10
Die lachet still und zieht sich heimlich
Fürsichtig die Pantoffeln aus.

Sie geht und weckt den Müllerburschen,
Der kaum den schweren Augen traut:
„Nun küsse mich, verliebter Junge; 15
Doch sauber, sauber, nicht zu laut."

105. Die Stadt

Am grauen Strand, am grauen Meer
Und seitab liegt die Stadt;
Der Nebel drückt die Dächer schwer,
Und durch die Stille braust das Meer
Eintönig um die Stadt. 5

Es rauscht kein Wald, es schlägt im Mai
Kein Vogel ohn' Unterlaß;
Die Wandergans mit hartem Schrei
Nur fliegt in Herbstesnacht vorbei,
Am Strande weht das Gras. 10

Doch hängt mein ganzes Herz an dir,
Du graue Stadt am Meer;
Der Jugend Zauber für und für
Ruht lächelnd doch auf dir, auf dir,
Du graue Stadt am Meer. 15

106. Über die Heide

Über die Heide hallet mein Schritt;
Dumpf aus der Erde wandert es mit.

Herbst ist gekommen, Frühling ist weit —
Gab es denn einmal selige Zeit?

5   Brauende Nebel geisten umher;
Schwarz ist das Kraut und der Himmel so leer.

Wär' ich hier nur nicht gegangen im Mai!
Leben und Liebe, — wie flog es vorbei!

107. Lucie

Ich seh sie noch, ihr Büchlein in der Hand,
Nach jener Bank dort an der Gartenwand
Vom Spiel der andern Kinder sich entfernen;
Sie wußte wohl, es mühte sie das Lernen.

5   Nicht war sie klug, nicht schön; mir aber war
Ihr blaß Gesichtchen und ihr blondes Haar,
Mir war es lieb; aus der Erinnrung Düster
Schaut es mich an; wir waren recht Geschwister.

Ihr schmales Bettchen teilte sie mit mir,
10   Und nächtens Wang' an Wange schliefen wir;
Das war so schön! Noch weht ein Kinderfrieden
Mich an aus jenen Zeiten, die geschieden.

Ein Ende kam; — ein Tag, sie wurde krank
Und lag im Fieber viele Wochen lang;
Ein Morgen dann, wo sanft die Winde gingen,   15
Da ging sie heim; es blühten die Syringen.

Die Sonne schien; ich lief ins Feld hinaus
Und weinte laut; dann kam ich still nach Haus.
Wohl zwanzig Jahr und drüber sind vergangen —
An wie viel andrem hat mein Herz gehangen!   20

Was hab' ich heute denn nach dir gebangt?
Bist du mir nah und hast nach mir verlangt?
Willst du, wie einst nach unsern Kinderspielen,
Mein Knabenhaupt an deinem Herzen fühlen?

108. Eine Frühlingsnacht

Im Zimmer drinnen ist's so schwül;
Der Kranke liegt auf dem heißen Pfühl.

Im Fieber hat er die Nacht verbracht;
Sein Herz ist müde, sein Auge verwacht.

Er lauscht auf der Stunden rinnenden Sand;   5
Er hält die Uhr in der weißen Hand.

Er zählt die Schläge, die sie pickt,
Er forschet, wie der Weiser rückt;

Es fragt ihn, ob er noch leb' vielleicht,
Wenn der Weiser die schwarze Drei erreicht.   10

Die Wartfrau sitzet geduldig dabei,
Harrend, bis alles vorüber sei. —

Schon auf dem Herzen drückt ihn der Tod;
Und draußen dämmert das Morgenrot.

15   An die Fenster klettert der Frühlingstag,
Mädchen und Vögel werden wach.

Die Erde lacht in Liebesschein,
Pfingstglocken läuten das Brautfest ein;

Singende Burschen ziehn übers Feld
20   Hinein in die blühende, klingende Welt. —

Und immer stiller wird es drin;
Die Alte tritt zum Kranken hin.

Der hat die Hände gefaltet dicht;
Sie zieht ihm das Laken übers Gesicht.

25   Dann geht sie fort. Stumm wird's und leer,
Und drinnen wacht kein Auge mehr.

109. April

Das ist die Drossel, die da schlägt,
Der Frühling, der mein Herz bewegt.
Ich fühle, die sich hold bezeigen,
Die Geister aus der Erde steigen.
5   Das Leben fließet wie ein Traum —
Mir ist wie Blume, Blatt und Baum.

110. Mai

Die Kinder schreien Vivat hoch!
In die blaue Luft hinein;
Den Frühling setzen sie auf den Thron.
Der soll ihr König sein.

*   *   *   *   *

Die Kinder haben die Veilchen gepflückt,   5
All, all, die da blühten am Mühlengraben.
Der Lenz ist da; sie wollen ihn fest
In ihren kleinen Fäusten haben.

111. Elisabeth

Meine Mutter hat's gewollt,
Den andern ich nehmen sollt';
Was ich zuvor besessen,
Mein Herz sollt es vergessen;
Das hat es nicht gewollt.   5

Meine Mutter klag' ich an,
Sie hat nicht wohl getan;
Was sonst in Ehren stünde,
Nun ist es worden Sünde.
Was fang' ich an?   10

Für all mein Stolz und Freud'
Gewonnen hab' ich Leid.
Ach, wär' das nicht geschehen,
Ach, könnt' ich betteln gehen
Über die braune Heid'!   15

112. Frauenhand

Ich weiß es wohl, kein klagend Wort
Wird über deine Lippen gehen;
Doch was so sanft dein Mund verschweigt,
Muß deine blasse Hand gestehen.

5   Die Hand, an der mein Auge hängt,
Zeigt jenen feinen Zug der Schmerzen,
Und daß in schlummerloser Nacht
Sie lag auf einem kranken Herzen.

113. Schließe mir die Augen beide

Schließe mir die Augen beide
Mit den lieben Händen zu!
Geht doch alles, was ich leide,
Unter deiner Hand zur Ruh'.
5   Und wie leise sich der Schmerz
Well' um Welle schlafen leget,
Wie der letzte Schlag sich reget,
Füllest du mein ganzes Herz.

Conrad Ferdinand Meyer

114. Liederseelen

In der Nacht, die die Bäume mit Blüten deckt,
Ward ich von süßen Gespenstern erschreckt,
Ein Reigen schwang im Garten sich,
Den ich mit leisem Fuß beschlich;
Wie zarter Elfen Chor im Ring   5
Ein weißer lebendiger Schimmer ging.
Die Schemen hab' ich keck befragt:
Wer seid ihr, luftige Wesen? Sagt!

„Ich bin ein Wölkchen, gespiegelt im See."
„Ich bin eine Reihe von Stapfen im Schnee."   10
„Ich bin ein Seufzer gen Himmel empor!"
„Ich bin ein Geheimnis, geflüstert ins Ohr."
„Ich bin ein frommes, gestorbnes Kind."
„Ich bin ein üppiges Blumengewind — "
„Und die du wählst, und der's beschied   15
Die Gunst der Stunde, die wird ein Lied."

115. Nachtgeräusche

Melde mir die Nachtgeräusche, Muse,
Die ans Ohr des Schlummerlosen fluten! —
Erst das traute Wachtgebell der Hunde,
Dann der abgezählte Schlag der Stunde,

5   Dann ein Fischer=Zwiegespräch am Ufer,
Dann? Nichts weiter als der ungewisse
Geisterlaut der ungebrochnen Stille,
Wie das Atmen eines jungen Busens,
Wie das Murmeln eines tiefen Brunnens,
10   Wie das Schlagen eines dumpfen Ruders,
Dann der ungehörte Tritt des Schlummers.

116. Das tote Kind

Es hat den Garten sich zum Freund gemacht,
Dann welkten er und es im Herbste sacht,
Die Sonne ging, und es und er entschlief,
Gehüllt in eine Decke weiß und tief.

5   Jetzt ist der Garten unversehns erwacht,
Die Kleine schlummert fest in ihrer Nacht.
„Wo steckst du?" summt es dort und summt es hier.
Der ganze Garten frägt nach ihr, nach ihr.

Die blaue Winde klettert schlank empor
10   Und blickt ins Haus: „Komm hinterm Schrank hervor!
Wo birgst du dich? Du tust dir's selbst zu leid!
Was hast du für ein neues Sommerkleid?"

117. Im Spätboot

Aus der Schiffsbank mach' ich meinen Pfühl,
Endlich wird die heiße Stirne kühl!
O wie süß erkaltet mir das Herz!
O wie weich verstummen Lust und Schmerz!

Über mir des Rohres schwarzer Rauch 5
Wiegt und biegt sich in des Windes Hauch.
Hüben hier und drüben wieder dort
Hält das Boot an manchem kleinen Port:
Bei der Schiffslaterne kargem Schein
Steigt ein Schatten aus und niemand ein. 10
Nur der Steurer noch, der wacht und steht!
Nur der Wind, der mir im Haare weht!
Schmerz und Lust erleiden sanften Tod.
Einen Schlumm'rer trägt das dunkle Boot.

118. Vor der Ernte

Am wolkenreinen Himmel geht
Die blanke Sichel schön,
Im Korne drunten wogt und weht
Und wühlt und rauscht der Föhn.

Sie wandert voller Melodie 5
Hochüber durch das Land.
Früh morgen schwingt die Schnitt'rin sie
Mit sonnenbrauner Hand.

119. Der römische Brunnen

Aufsteigt der Strahl und fallend gießt
Er voll der Marmorschale Rund,
Die, sich verschleiernd, überfließt
In einer zweiten Schale Grund;

5 Die zweite gibt, sie wird zu reich,
   Der dritten wallend ihre Flut,
   Und jede nimmt und gibt zugleich
      Und strömt und ruht.

120. Neujahrsglocken

In den Lüften schwellendes Gedröhne,
Leicht wie Halme biegt der Wind die Töne:

Leis' verhallen, die zum ersten riefen,
Neu Geläute hebt sich aus den Tiefen.

5 Große Heere, nicht ein einzler Rufer!
   Wohllaut flutet ohne Strand und Ufer.

121. Säerspruch

Bemeßt der Schritt! Bemeßt den Schwung!
Die Erde bleibt noch lange jung!
Dort fällt ein Korn, das stirbt und ruht.
Die Ruh' ist süß. Es hat es gut.
5 Hier eins das durch die Scholle bricht.
Es hat es gut. Süß ist das Licht.
Und keines fällt aus dieser Welt
Und jedes fällt, wie 's Gott gefällt.

122. Schnitterlied

Wir schnitten die Saaten, wir Buben und Dirnen,
Mit nackenden Armen und triefenden Stirnen,
Von donnernden dunklen Gewittern bedroht —
Gerettet das Korn und nicht einer, der darbe!
    Von Garbe zu Garbe 5
    Ist Raum für den Tod —
Wie schwellen die Lippen des Lebens so rot!

Hoch thronet ihr Schönen auf güldenen Sitzen,
In strotzenden Garben umflimmert von Blitzen —
Nicht eine, die darbe! Wir bringen das Brot! 10
Zum Reigen! Zum Tanze! Zur tosenden Runde!
    Von Munde zu Munde
    Ist Raum für den Tod —
Wie schwellen die Lippen des Lebens so rot!

123. Nach einem Niederländer

Der Meister malt ein kleines zartes Bild,
Zurückgelehnt, beschaut er's liebevoll.
Es pocht. „Herein." Ein flämischer Junker ist's.
Mit einer drallen, aufgedonnerten Dirn',
Der vor Gesundheit fast die Wange birst. 5
Sie rauscht von Seide, flimmert von Geschmeid.
„Wir haben's eilig, lieber Meister. Wißt,
Ein wackrer Schelm stiehlt mir das Töchterlein.
Morgen ist Hochzeit. Malet mir mein Kind!"
„Zur Stunde, Herr! Nur noch den Pinselstrich!" 10
Sie treten lustig vor die Staffelei:

Auf einem blanken Kissen schlummernd liegt
Ein feiner Mädchenkopf. Der Meister setzt
Des Blumenkranzes tiefste Knospe noch
15 Auf die verblichne Stirn mit leichter Hand.
— „Nach der Natur?" — „Nach der Natur. Mein Kind.
Gestern beerdigt. Herr, ich bin zu Dienst."

124. Eingelegte Ruder

Meine eingelegten Ruder triefen,
Tropfen fallen langsam in die Tiefen.

Nichts, das mich verdroß! Nichts, das mich freute!
Niederrinnt ein schmerzenloses Heute!

5   Unter mir — ach, aus dem Licht verschwunden —
Träumen schon die schönern meiner Stunden.

Aus der blauen Tiefe ruft das Gestern:
Sind im Licht noch manche meiner Schwestern?

125. Ewig jung ist nur die Sonne

Heute fanden meine Schritte mein vergeßnes Jugendtal,
Seine Sohle lag verödet, seine Berge standen kahl.
Meine Bäume, meine Träume, meine buchendunkeln Höh'n —
Ewig jung ist nur die Sonne, sie allein ist ewig schön.

5 Drüben dort in schilf'gem Grunde, wo die müde Lache liegt,
Hat zu meiner Jugendstunde sich lebend'ge Flut gewiegt,
Durch die Heiden, durch die Weiden ging ein wandernd
        Herdgetön —
Ewig jung ist nur die Sonne, sie allein ist ewig schön.

126. Requiem

Bei der Abendsonne Wandern
Wann ein Dorf den Strahl verlor,
Klagt sein Dunkel es den andern
Mit vertrauten Tönen vor.

Noch ein Glöcklein hat geschwiegen   5
Auf der Höhe bis zuletzt.
Nun beginnt es sich zu wiegen,
Horch, mein Kilchberg läutet jetzt!

127. Abendwolke

So stille ruht im Hafen
Das tiefe Wasser dort,
Die Ruder sind entschlafen,
Die Schifflein sind im Port.

Nur oben in dem Äther   5
Der lauen Maiennacht,
Dort segelt noch ein später
Friedfert'ger Ferge sacht.

Die Barke still und dunkel
Fährt hin im Dämmerschein   10
Und leisem Sterngefunkel
Am Himmel und hinein.

128. Das Glöcklein

Er steht an ihrem Pfühl in herber Qual,
Den jungen Busen muß er keuchen sehn —
Er ist ein Arzt. Er weiß, sein traut Gemahl
Erblaßt, sobald die Morgenschauer wehn.

5 Sie hat geschlummert: „Lieber, du bei mir?
Mir träumte, daß ich auf der Alpe war,
Wie schön mir träumte, das erzähl' ich dir —
Du schickst mich wieder hin das nächste Jahr!

Dort vor dem Dorf — du weißt den moos'gen Stein —
10 Saß ich umhallt von lauter Herdgetön,
An mir vorüber zogen mit Schalmei'n
Die Herden nieder von den Sommerhöh'n.

Die Herden kehren alle heut nach Haus —
Das ist die letzte wohl? Nein, eine noch:
15 Noch ein Geläut klingt an und eins klingt aus!
Das endet nicht! Da kam das letzte doch!

Mich überflutete das Abendrot,
Die Matten dunkelten so grün und rein,
Die Firnen brannten aus und waren tot,
20 Darüber glomm ein leiser Sternenschein —

Du horch! ein Glöcklein läutet in der Schlucht,
Verirrt, verspätet, wandert's ohne Ruh,
Ein armes Glöcklein, das die Herde sucht —
Aufwacht' ich dann, und bei mir warest du!

O bring mich wieder auf die lieben Höh'n —   25
Sie haben, sagst du, mich gesund gemacht . . .
Dort war es schön! Dort war es wunderschön!
Das Glöcklein! Wieder! Hörst du's? Gute Nacht. . . ."

129. Die Bank des Alten

Ich bin einmal in einem Tal gegangen,
Das fern der Welt, dem Himmel nahe war,
Durch das Gelände seiner Wiesen klangen
Die Sensen rings der zweiten Mahd im Jahr.

Ich schritt durch eines Dörfchens stille Gassen.   5
Kein Laut. Vor einer Hütte saß allein
Ein alter Mann, von seiner Kraft verlassen,
Und schaute feiernd auf den Firneschein.

Zuweilen, in die Hand gelegt die Stirne,
Seh' ich den Himmel jenes Tales blau,   10
Den Müden seh ich wieder auf die Firne,
Die nahen, selig klaren Firnen schaun.

's ist nur ein Traum. Wohl ist der Greis geschieden
Aus dieser Sonne Licht von Jahren schwer;
Er schlummert wohl in seines Grabes Frieden,   15
Und seine Bank steht vor der Hütte leer.

Noch pulst mein Leben feurig. Wie den andern
Kommt mir ein Tag, da mich die Kraft verrät;
Dann will ich langsam in die Berge wandern
Und suchen, wo die Bank des Alten steht.   20

Detlev von Liliencron

130. Die Musik kommt

Klingling, bumbum und tschingdada,
Zieht im Triumph der Perserschah?
Und um die Ecke brausend bricht's
Wie Tubaton des Weltgerichts,
5   Voran der Schellenträger.

Brumbrum, das große Bombardon,
Der Beckenschlag, das Helikon,
Die Piccolo, der Zinkenist,
Die Türkentrommel, der Flötist,
10   Und dann der Herre Hauptmann.

Der Hauptmann naht mit stolzem Sinn,
Die Schuppenkette unterm Kinn,
Die Schärpe schnürt den schlanken Leib,
Beim Zeus! das ist kein Zeitvertreib,
15   Und dann die Herren Leutnants.

Zwei Leutnants, rosenrot und braun,
Die Fahne schützen sie als Zaun,
Die Fahne kommt, den Hut nimm ab,
Der bleiben treu wir bis ans Grab!
20   Und dann die Grenadiere.

Der Grenadier im strammen Tritt,
In Schritt und Tritt und Tritt und Schritt,
Das stampft und dröhnt und klappt und flirrt,
Laternenglas und Fenster klirrt,
    Und dann die kleinen Mädchen.   25

Die Mädchen alle, Kopf an Kopf,
Das Auge blau und blond der Zopf,
Aus Tür und Tor und Hof und Haus
Schaut Mine, Trine, Stine aus,
    Vorbei ist die Musike.   30

Klingling, tschingtsching und Paukenkrach,
Noch aus der Ferne tönt es schwach,
Ganz leise bumbumbumbum tsching;
Zog da ein bunter Schmetterling,
    Tschingtsching, bum, um die Ecke?   35

131. Tod in Ähren

Im Weizenfeld, in Korn und Mohn,
Liegt ein Soldat, unaufgefunden,
Zwei Tage schon, zwei Nächte schon,
Mit schweren Wunden, unverbunden.

Durstüberquält und fieberwild,   5
Im Todeskampf den Kopf erhoben.
Ein letzter Traum, ein letztes Bild,
Sein brechend Auge schlägt nach oben.

Die Sense sirrt im Ährenfeld,
10   Er sieht sein Dorf im Arbeitsfrieden,
Ade, ade du Heimatwelt —
Und beugt das Haupt, und ist verschieden.

132. In Erinnerung

Wilde Rosen überschlugen
Tiefer Wunden rotes Blut.
Windverwehte Klänge trugen
Siegesmarsch und Siegesflut.

5   Nacht. Entsetzen überspülte
Dorf und Dach in Lärm und Glut.
„Wasser!" Und die Hand zerwühlte
Gras und Staub in Dursteswut.

Morgen. Gräbergraber. Grüfte.
10   Manch ein letzter Atemzug.
Weither, witternd, durch die Lüfte
Braust und graust ein Geierflug.

133. Wer weiß wo

(Schlacht bei Kolin, 18. Juni 1757.)

Auf Blut und Leichen, Schutt und Qualm,
Auf roßzerstampften Sommerhalm
Die Sonne schien.

Es sank die Nacht. Die Schlacht ist aus,
Und mancher kehrte nicht nach Haus   5
Einst von Kolin.

Ein Junker auch, ein Knabe noch,
Der heut das erste Pulver roch,
Er mußte dahin.
Wie hoch er auch die Fahne schwang,   10
Der Tod in seinen Arm ihn zwang,
Er mußte dahin.

Ihm nahe lag ein frommes Buch,
Das stets der Junker bei sich trug
Am Degenknauf.   15
Ein Grenadier von Bevern fand
Den kleinen erdbeschmutzten Band
Und hob ihn auf.

Und brachte heim mit schnellem Fuß
Dem Vater diesen letzten Gruß,   20
Der klang nicht froh.
Dann schrieb hinein die Zitterhand:
„Kolin. Mein Sohn verscharrt im Sand.
Wer weiß wo.“

Und der gesungen dieses Lied,   25
Und der es liest, im Leben zieht
Noch frisch und froh.
Doch einst bin ich, und bist auch du,
Verscharrt im Sand, zur ewigen Ruh',
Wer weiß wo.   30

134. Sommernacht

An ferne Berge schlug die Donnerkeulen
Ein rasch verrauschtes Nachmittaggewitter.
Die Bauern zogen heim auf müden Gäulen,
Und singend kehrten Winzervolk und Schnitter.
5 Auf allen Dächern qualmten blaue Säulen
Genügsam himmelan, ein luftig Gitter.
Nun ist es Nacht, es geistern schon die Eulen,
Einsam aus einer Laube klingt die Zither.

135. Meiner Mutter

Wie oft sah ich die blassen Hände nähen,
Ein Stück für mich — wie liebevoll du sorgtest!
Ich sah zum Himmel deine Augen flehen,
Ein Wunsch für mich — wie liebevoll du sorgtest!
5 Und an mein Bett kamst du mit leisen Zehen,
Ein Schutz für mich — wie sorgenvoll du horchtest!
Längst schon dein Grab die Winde überwehen,
Ein Gruß für mich — wie liebevoll du sorgtest!

136. Wiegenlied

Vor der Türe schläft der Baum,
Durch den Garten zieht ein Traum.
Langsam schwimmt der Mondeskahn,
Und im Schlafe kräht der Hahn.
5   Schlaf, mein Wölfchen, schlaf.

Schlaf, mein Wulff. In später Stund
Küss' ich deinen roten Mund.
Streck dein kleines dickes Bein,
Steht noch nicht auf Weg und Stein.
    Schlaf, mein Wölfchen, schlaf.   10

Schlaf, mein Wulff. Es kommt die Zeit,
Regen rinnt, es stürmt und schneit.
Lebst in atemloser Hast,
Hättest gerne Schlaf und Rast.
    Schlaf, mein Wölfchen, schlaf.   15

Vor der Türe steht der Baum,
Durch den Garten zieht ein Traum.
Langsam schwimmt der Mondeskahn,
Und im Schlafe kräht der Hahn.
    Schlaf, mein Wölfchen, schlaf.   20

137. Viererzug

Vorne vier nickende Pferdeköpfe,
Neben mir zwei blonde Mädchenzöpfe,
Hinten der Groom mit wichtigen Mienen,
An den Rädern Gebell.

In den Dörfern windstillen Lebens Genüge,   5
Auf den Feldern fleißige Spaten und Pflüge,
Alles das von der Sonne beschienen
So hell, so hell.

138. Schöne Junitage

Mitternacht, die Gärten lauschen,
Flüsterwort und Liebeskuß,
Bis der letzte Klang verklungen,
Weil nun alles schlafen muß —
5   Flußüberwärts singt eine Nachtigall.

Sonnengrüner Rosengarten,
Sonnenweiße Stromesflut,
Sonnenstiller Morgenfriede,
Der auf Baum und Beeten ruht —
10   Flußüberwärts singt eine Nachtigall.

Straßentreiben, fern, verworren,
Reicher Mann und Bettelkind,
Myrtenkränze, Leichenzüge,
Tausendfältig Leben rinnt —
15   Flußüberwärts singt eine Nachtigall.

Langsam graut der Abend nieder,
Milde wird die harte Welt,
Und das Herz macht seinen Frieden,
Und zum Kinde wird der Held —
20   Flußüberwärts singt eine Nachtigall.

Richard Dehmel

139. Der Arbeitsmann

Wir haben ein Bett, wir haben ein Kind, mein Weib!
Wir haben auch Arbeit, und gar zu zweit,
Und haben die Sonne und Regen und Wind,
Und uns fehlt nur eine Kleinigkeit,
Um so frei zu sein, wie die Vögel sind: 5
Nur Zeit.

Wenn wir Sonntags durch die Felder gehn, mein Kind,
Und über den Ähren weit und breit
Das blaue Schwalbenvolk blitzen sehn,
O, dann fehlt uns nicht das bißchen Kleid,   10
Um so schön zu sein, wie die Vögel sind:
Nur Zeit.

Nur Zeit! wir wittern Gewitterwind, wir Volk.
Nur eine kleine Ewigkeit;
Uns fehlt ja nichts, mein Weib, mein Kind,   15
Als all das, was durch uns gedeiht,
Um so kühn zu sein, wie die Vögel sind.
Nur Zeit.

140. Die stille Stadt

Liegt eine Stadt im Tale,
Ein blasser Tag vergeht;
Es wird nicht lange dauern mehr,
Bis weder Mond noch Sterne,
5   Nur Nacht am Himmel steht.

Von allen Bergen drücken
Nebel auf die Stadt;
Es dringt kein Dach, nicht Hof noch Haus,
Kein Laut aus ihrem Rauch heraus,
10   Kaum Türme noch und Brücken.

Doch als den Wandrer graute,
Da ging ein Lichtlein auf im Grund;
Und durch den Rauch und Nebel
Begann ein leiser Lobgesang
15   Aus Kindermund.

141. Dann

Wenn der Regen durch die Gosse tropft,
Bei Nacht, du liegst und horchst hinaus,
Kein Mensch kann ins Haus,
Du liegst allein,
5   Allein: O käm' er doch! Da klopft
Es, klopft, laut — hörst du? — leise, schwach
Tönt's im Uhrgehäuse nach;
Dann tritt Totenstille ein.

142. Manche Nacht

Wenn die Felder sich verdunkeln,
Fühl' ich, wird mein Auge heller;
Schon versucht ein Stern zu funkeln,
Und die Grillen wispern schneller.

Jeder Laut wird bilderreicher,   5
Das Gewohnte sonderbarer,
Hintern Wald der Himmel bleicher,
Jeder Wipfel hebt sich klarer.

Und du merkst es nicht im Schreiten,
Wie das Licht verhundertfältigt   10
Sich entringt den Dunkelheiten.
Plötzlich stehst du überwältigt.

143. Nacht für Nacht

Still, es ist ein Tag verflossen.
Deine Augen sind geschlossen.
Deine Hände, schwer wie Blei,
Liegen dir so drückend ferne.
Um dein Bette schweben Sterne,   5
Dicht an dir vorbei.

Still, sie weiten dir die Wände:
Gib uns her die schweren Hände,
Sieh, der dunkle Himmel weicht —
Deine Augen sind geschlossen —   10
Still, du hast den Tag genossen —
Dir wird leicht.

144. Befreit

Du wirst nicht weinen. Leise, leise
Wirst du lächeln; und wie zur Reise
Geb ich dir Blick und Kuß zurück.
Unsre lieben vier Wände! Du hast sie bereitet,
5   Ich habe sie dir zur Welt geweitet —
O Glück!

Dann wirst du heiß meine Hände fassen
Und wirst mir deine Seele lassen,
Läßt unsern Kindern mich zurück.
10   Du schenktest mir dein ganzes Leben,
Ich will es ihnen wiedergeben —
O Glück!

Es wird sehr bald sein, wir wissen's beide,
Wir haben einander befreit vom Leide;
15   So geb' ich dich der Welt zurück.
Dann wirst du mir nur noch im Traum erscheinen
Und mich segnen und mit mir weinen —
O Glück!

145. Gleichnis

Es ist ein Brunnen, der heißt Leid;
Draus fließt die lautre Seligkeit.
Doch wer nur in den Brunnen schaut,
Den graut.

Er sieht im tiefen Wasserschacht 5
Sein lichtes Bild umrahmt von Nacht.
O trinke! da zerrinnt dein Bild:
Licht quillt.

146. Hochsommerlied

Golden streift der Sommer meine Heimat,
Brotwarm schwillt das hohe reife Korn,
Wie in meiner goldnen Kinderzeit;
Habe Dank, geliebte Erde!

Schwalben rufen mich hinaus ins Blaue, 5
Weiße Wolken türmen Glanz auf Glanz,
Wie in meiner blauen Jünglingszeit;
Habe Dank, geliebte Sonne!

STEFAN GEORGE

147. Die Spange

Ich wollte sie aus kühlem eisen
Und wie ein glatter fester streif
Doch war im schacht auf allen gleisen
So kein metall zum gusse reif.

5   Nun aber soll sie also sein:
Wie eine grosse fremde dolde
Geformt aus feuerrotem golde
Und reichem blitzendem gestein.

148. Der Einsiedel

Ins offne fenster nickten die hollunder
Die ersten reben standen in der bluht'
Da kam mein sohn zurück vom land der wunder'
Da hat mein sohn an meiner brust geruht.

5   Ich liess mir allen seinen kummer beichten'
Gekränkten stolz auf seinem erden-ziehn —
Ich hätte ihm so gerne meinen leichten
Und sichern frieden hier bei mir verliehn.

Doch anders fügten es der himmel sorgen —
10   Sie nahmen nicht mein reiches lösegeld . .
Er ging an einem jungen ruhmes-morgen'
Ich sah nur fern noch seinen schild im feld.

149.

Wir schreiten auf und ab im reichen flitter
Des buchenganges beinah bis zum tore
Und sehen aussen in dem feld vom gitter
Den mandelbaum zum zweitenmal im flore.

Wir suchen nach den schattenfreien bänken   5
Dort wo uns niemals fremde Stimmen scheuchten'
In träumen unsre arme sich verschränken'
Wir laben uns am langen milden leuchten.

Wir fühlen dankbar wie zu leisem brausen
Von wipfeln strahlenspuren auf uns tropfen   10
Und blicken nur und horchen wenn in pausen
Die reifen früchte an den boden klopfen.

150.

Ihr tratet zu dem herde
Wo alle glut verstarb'
Licht war nur an der erde
Vom monde leichenfarb.

Ihr tauchtet in die aschen   '5
Die bleichen finger ein
Mit suchen tasten haschen —
Wird es noch einmal schein!

Seht was mit trostgebärde
Der mond euch rät: 10
Tretet weg vom herde
Es ist worden spät.

151. Das Licht

Wir sind in trauer wenn' uns minder günstig
Du dich zu andren' mehr beglückten' drehst
Wenn unser geist' nach anbetungen brünstig'
An abenden in deinem abglanz wes't.

5 Wir wären töricht' wollten wir dich hassen
Wenn oft dein strahl verderbendrohend sticht
Wir wären kinder' wollten wir dich fassen —
Da du für alle leuchtest' süsses Licht!

Rainer Maria Rilke

152.

Die armen Worte, die im Alltag darben,
Die unscheinbaren Worte, lieb ich so.
Aus meinen Festen schenk' ich ihnen Farben,
Da lächeln sie und werden langsam froh.

Ihr Wesen, das sie bang in sich bezwangen,   5
Erneut sich deutlich, daß es jeder sieht;
Sie sind noch niemals im Gesang gegangen,
Und schauernd schreiten sie in meinem Lied.

153. Der Panther

Im Jardin des Plantes, Paris

Sein Blick ist vom Vorübergehn der Stäbe
So müd geworden, daß er nichts mehr hält.
Ihm ist, als ob es tausend Stäbe gäbe
Und hinter tausend Stäben keine Welt.

Der weiche Gang geschmeidig starker Schritte,   5
Der sich im allerkleinsten Kreise dreht,
Ist wie ein Tanz von Kraft um eine Mitte,
In der betäubt ein großer Wille steht.

Nur manchmal schiebt der Vorhang der Pupille
10   Sich lautlos auf —. Dann geht ein Bild hinein,
Geht durch der Glieder angespannte Stille —
Und hört im Herzen auf zu sein.

154. Die Erblindende

Sie saß so wie die anderen beim Tee.
Mir war zuerst, als ob sie ihre Tasse
Ein wenig anders als die andern fasse.
Sie lächelte einmal. Es tat fast weh.

5   Und als man schließlich sich erhob und sprach
Und langsam und wie es der Zufall brachte
Durch viele Zimmer ging (man sprach und lachte),
Da sah ich sie. Sie ging den andern nach,

Verhalten, so wie eine, welche gleich
10   Wird singen müssen und vor vielen Leuten;
Auf ihren hellen Augen, die sich freuten,
War Licht von außen wie auf einem Teich.

Sie folgte langsam, und sie brauchte lang,
Als wäre etwas noch nicht überstiegen;
15   Und doch: als ob, nach einem Übergang,
Sie nicht mehr gehen würde, sondern fliegen.

155.

Du mußt das Leben nicht verstehen,
Dann wird es werden wie ein Fest.
Und laß dir jeden Tag geschehen,
So wie ein Kind im Weitergehen
Von jedem Wehen   5
Sich viele Blüten schenken läßt.

Sie aufzusammeln und zu sparen,
Das kommt dem Kind nicht in den Sinn.
Es löst sie leise aus den Haaren,
Drin sie so gern gefangen waren,   10
Und hält den lieben jungen Jahren
Nach neuen seine Hände hin.

156. Widmung

Schwer ist zu Gott der Abstieg. Aber schau:
Du müßt dich ab mit deinen leeren Krügen,
Und plötzlich ist doch: Kind sein, Mädchen, Frau —
Ausreichend, um ihm endlos zu genügen.

Er ist das Wasser: bilde du nur rein   5
Die Schale aus zwei hingewillten Händen,
Und kniest du überdies —: er wird verschwenden
Und deiner größten Fassung über sein.

A WORD TO THE READER

Verse must be read aloud. Rhyme, rhythm, alliteration, assonance, vowel coloring, the effect of enjambement, to name only the more obvious phenomena, appeal solely to the ear. Looking at a page of verse is like looking at a page of music. Unless the symbols are translated into sound values, the effect is blank. A skilled musician is able to translate the printed notes to the inner sense, but even he will prefer to hear the music and will always consider this the final test. Thus it is also with verse: it must be read aloud. Lyric verse is best read in privacy or in a small congenial group. When the humdrum noise and the humdrum cares of the world have vanished, then the moment has come when one may steep one's soul in lyric beauty. One never tires of a really great lyric: like a true friend, a longer acquaintance adds only new delight.

And why read lyric poetry at all? Some people ask that question, and for them the case may be hopeless. If the lyric sense is utterly lacking, then it is their sad lot to live in the desert of the practical world. Art is not for them: neither music nor poetry nor painting nor sculpture nor architecture; for something of the lyric impulse lives in all of these. But many ask that question who some day will see, and for them I must attempt a brief answer. All literature is an interpretation of life, and the better one understands life the better one understands literature, and vice versa. Lyric poetry is the most direct interpretation of life, because here the poet reveals his innermost self directly. We strive to enrich our intellectual power by reliving the thought of Plato and of Kant. Why not enrich our emotional life and our whole being by reliving the world of Goethe or Shelley? The poets have lived for us, and the pure essence of their life we can make our own in their lyric verse.

ELEMENTS OF VERSIFICATION

RHYTHM. — While in Greek and Latin it depends on quantity, i.e., length of the syllables, in German as in English it depends on stress, that is, accent. The smallest rhythmical unit is called a foot and corresponds to a measure in music with the exception that the accent need not be on the first syllable. A verse consists of two or more feet (verses with only a single foot are rare) and may end either with an accented syllable (masculine ending) or with an unaccented (feminine ending). Especially within longer verses there often occurs a slight rest or break, called caesura. Designating the accented syllable by — and the unaccented by ×, the more common feet with their Graeco-Roman names may be represented thus:

Iambus, × —
Trochee, — ×
Dactyl, — × ×
Anapaest, × × —.

This terminology is, however, of little avail in the German Volkslied, that is the simple folksong, and in that large body of German verse which is patterned after it. Here the basic principle is the number of accented syllables. The number of unaccented syllables varies. A measure (i.e., a foot) may have either one or two unaccented syllables, in the real Volkslied often three. (A measure without an unaccented syllable, so common in older verse, is but rarely met with to-day; see **84**, 7.) Goethe's more popular ballads as Erlkönig or der König in Thule offer good examples of this freer technique. Above all, however, Heine made use of this principle, while Platen, whom later German verse tends to follow in this respect (e.g., Meyer and Liliencron), espoused the strict classic ideal.[1]

RHYME. — When two or more words correspond from their accented vowel on, they are said to rhyme: Pferde — Erde. The rhyming syllable must carry at least a secondary accent:

[1] Exceptions are only apparent, as in **68**, 7. Platen followed the rules of Graeco-Roman prosody, where a long syllable could be substituted for two short syllables.

Heiligkeit — Zeit. Rhymes of one syllable are called **masculine,** of two syllables feminine. According to their degree of **perfection** rhymes are classified as pure and impure. Thus geboren — geschworen, bestellt — Welt are pure, gesehn — schön, gerissen — Füßen, Lied — Gemüt, sprach — Gemach, Wiesen — fließen are impure. Impure rhymes are not of necessity poor, but may be used to enhance the musical effects of a poem. Heine was a master in this respect. The modern school, however, tends to avoid impure rhymes.

Rhymes within a verse are called internal rhymes.

ALLITERATION — two or more accented syllables beginning with the same consonant or with a vowel: Von weißen Wolken umwogt, **59,** 2 — is used to enhance the rhythmic-melodic character of a poem, as is also assonance — the agreement of vowels in two or more accented syllables, **36.** Often assonance is practically a form of impure rhyme, Grunde — verschwunden, **41,** Himmel — Schimmer, **44.**

STANZA — a union of two or more verses. In a stanza itself the individual verses may either stand apart or two or more verses may form larger units. Thus the structure of the various stanzas may be made to differentiate and the rhythmic-melodic character of the poem be thereby modified (**44 and 56** and notes). Similarly, stanzas may form larger units (**2**). If the end of a verse breaks into a syntactic unit, we have what is called an enjambement. This tends to put a special stress on the last word. Notice for example the onomatopoetic effect in **13,** 7 and 8:

> Aus dem bewegten Wasser rauscht
> Ein feuchtes Weib hervor.

REFRAIN. — This is a repetition of one or more verses, either exactly repeated or slightly modified, at the end of a stanza or less frequently at another fixed place (**4, 10, 34**). Aside from its rhythmic-melodic effect the refrain helps to center the attention on a certain idea or motif.

STANZA AND VERSE FORMS. — Only a few need any special discussion.

1. *Blank Verse.* This is the verse of Shakspere and was

introduced into Germany from England. It is an unrhymed iambic verse of five feet (**19**).

2. *Freie Rhythmen.* An unrhymed verse that does not follow any fixed form; the rhythm may vary even within the verse. The number of accented syllables usually does not exceed four (**15, 16** and **59**).

3. *The Rhymed Couplet* (vierhebige Reimpaare) was introduced from the Volkslied. The verse ending is always masculine. Best adapted to a rapidly progressing action, every stanza marks a forward step, portrays a new scene (**28, 29, 74**).

4. *The Sonnet*, an Italian verse form, is composed of fourteen iambic lines of five feet each. The rhyme for the first eight lines, called the octave, is always *abbaabba;* for the last six, called the sestette, the rhyme may be *cdcdcd, ccdccd,* or *cdecde* (**69** and **77**).

5. *The Siziliane*, likewise Italian, consists of eight iambic lines of five feet each, the rhyme being *abababab* (**135** and **136**).

6. *The Modified Nibelungen Stanza*, an adaptation of the stanza of the Nibelungenlied introduced by Uhland, is a stanza of four verses rhyming in couplets; each verse has six accented syllables with a fixed pause as indicated below in the scansion of the first two lines of **32:**

$$\times - \times - \times - \times \mid\mid \times - \times - \times -$$
$$\times - \times -\times\times - \times \mid\mid \times - \times - \times -$$

Each line is in reality composed of two verses and thus we have here the form so commonly used by Heine (**48, 49, 50, 51, 52** and others). Each verse has in reality four measures, the last measure being taken up by a pause:

Es stand in al ten Zei ten | | ein Schloß so hoch und hehr.

$$\times \ - \ \times - \times \ - \ \times \ \P \quad \times \ - \ \times - \times \ - \ \P$$

In music these pauses may be taken up in whole or in part by lengthening the preceding notes (to some extent this holds true in reading, adding to the effect of the enjambement). Die Lorelei offers a good example:

Ich weiß nicht, was soll es be = deu = ten, daß ich so trau=rig bin; ein Mär=chen aus al = ten Zei = ten, das kommt mir nicht aus dem Sinn. Die Luft ist kühl und es dun=kelt, und ru = hig fließt der Rhein; der Gip=fel des Ber=ges fun = kelt im A = bend=son=nen=schein.

NOTES

GOETHE

Johann Wolfgang von Goethe, the world's greatest lyric genius, was born August 28, 1749, in Frankfurt am Main. In his being there were happily blended his mother's joyous fancy and the sterner traits of his father. Thus a rich imagination, a wealth of feeling, and the power of poetic expression went hand in hand with an indomitable will. In the spring of 1770 the young poet went to Strassburg to complete his law course. There Herder happened to be, even then a famed critic and scholar, and he aroused in Goethe a love and understanding of what was really great and genuine in literature: especially Homer, the Bible, Shakspere, and the Volfslied i.e., the simple folksong. In the fall of the year Goethe met Friederike Brion in the parsonage at Sesenheim, a village near Strassburg. Now Herder's teaching bore fruit in an outburst of real song (**1, 2** and **4**). The influence of the Volfslied is clearly discernible in the unaffected naturalness, spontaneity, and simplicity of these lyrics. Thus das Heidenröslein, which symbolizes the tragic close of the sweet idyll of Sesenheim, is to all intents and purposes a Volfslied.

The following years, spent for the most part in Frankfurt, were the period of Sturm und Drang (Storm and Stress) in the poet's life and work. His love for Lili Schönemann, a rich banker's daughter and society belle of Frankfurt, only heightened this unrest (**3**). In the fall of 1775 the young duke Karl August called Goethe to Weimar. Under the influence of Frau von Stein, a woman of rare culture, Goethe developed to calm maturity. Compare the first Wanderers Nachtlied (written February 1776), a passionate prayer for peace, and the second (written September 1780), the embodiment of that peace attained. Even more important in this development is the fact that Goethe, in assuming his many official positions in the little dukedom, entered voluntarily a circle of everyday duties (**7** and **8**). Thus the heaven-storming Titan, as Goethe reveals himself in his *Prometheus*, learns to respect and revere the natural limitations of mortality (**15** and especially **16**).

As Goethe matured, his affinity for classic antiquity became more marked, and a consuming desire impelled him to spend two years in Italy (1786–1788). The rest of his years Goethe spent in Weimar, his life enriched above all else by his friendship with Schiller. In this second Weimar period Goethe reached the acme of his powers. Even his declining years, although marked by loneliness and bringing him a full measure of grief (his wife, Christiane Vulpius, whom he had met shortly after his return from Italy, died in 1816, followed in 1830 by his only son), exemplified that earnest striving so characteristic of Goethe. A serene optimism, a deep love of life, was his to the very last. To this das Lied des Türmers, written May 1831, bears eloquent witness. A ripe mellowness seems to blend here with the joyous spirit of youth. Goethe died March 22, 1832.

1. A visit to Sesenheim is the experience that called forth this poem. (Compare Goethe's first letter to Friederike, October 15, 1770.) Notice how all nature is personified and assumes human attributes. In the opening stanzas impetuous haste is stirring, the first two lines have a marked rising rhythm. Notice the quieting effect of the metrical inversion at the beginning of 17, 18, and 19 and of the break in 25 after ад and how the whole poem ends with a note of deep joy.

15, 16. welches, welche = *what*.

21. rofenfarbnes Frühlingswetter, *the roseate hues of spring-time.*

29. Erben, old dative singular.

2. Notice that the second and third stanzas are joined as also the last three. The exuberant fullness of joy creates its own form and overleaps the confines of a single stanza.

3. Written June 1775 in Switzerland on Lake Zürich. Goethe had gone there to escape the unrest into which his love for Lili Schönemann had thrown him. The poem opens with a shout of exultation, 1 and 2; note the inversion —×× —× — Saug' id aus freier Welt. The rising rhythm of the following lines clearly depicts the movement of rapid rowing. Stanza 2 changes to a falling rhythm; as pictures of the past rise up, the rowing ceases. Stanza 3 depicts a more quiet forward movement; notice the effect of the dactyls in the even lines.

15. trinfen, metaphorically for *envelop, cause to disappear.*

4. The refrain, so common in the Volfslied does not only enhance the melody of the poem, but centers the entire attention on das Röslein and retards the quick dramatic movement of the narrative, which latter is heightened by the omission of the article and the frequent inversion of the verb.

2. Heiden, old dative.

3. morgenschön, the rose has all the fresh pure beauty of the early morning.

18. Weh und Ad, *cry of pain, piteous outcry.*

5. For this and the following poem compare Longfellow's translation.

6. Ein gleiches, i.e., another Wanderers Nachtlied. This poem has been justly called die Krone aller Lyrik, *the acme of all lyric poetry*, because of its simple, perfect beauty.

8. Erinnerung, *reminder*.

9. Written in 1813 in memory of the twenty-fifth anniversary of the day when the poet had first met Christiane Vulpius. Its never failing charm lies in its utter simplicity, its Selbstverständlichkeit, and in this one respect it may well be compared to Wordsworth's Lucy (" She dwelt among the untrodden ways ").

1 and 2. Für sich (i.e., vor sich) hingehen, *to saunter along, to walk along without any special purpose.*

10. Mignon, a fascinating character in Goethe's novel Wilhelm Meister, a strangely precocious child, expresses in this song her longing for her Italian land. In succinct pictures there arise before us her native land, her ancestral home and the way thither. The very soul of this poem is longing, culminating with ever increasing intensity in the refrain. Note the vivid concreteness of the verbs and the noble simplicity of the adjectives; the vowels, especially in 2.

13. Wolkensteg, *bridge that hangs on clouds* (Carlyle).

16. stürzt, *plunges down*, i.e., descends precipitously.

11. The Harfenspieler has, without knowing it, married his own sister. Mignon is the child of this union. In this song he pours forth his despair and the torments of his conscience.

12. Thule is a mythical land of the far North.

3. sterbend modifies Buhle.

7. *his eyes overflowed with tears.*

8. so oft, *as often as.*

12. zugleich, i.e., with his other possessions.

15. auf, translate *in*. Why auf?

21, 22. Note the descriptive effect of the enjambement together with the internal rhyme.

23. *His eyes closed* (in death). **Täten sinken = sanken.** **Täten** is an older preterite indicative.

13. The poem embodies the lure of the water. This motif is clearly expressed in 1 and is repeated in 25. In 9, 13, 29 and 31 metrically the same motif recurs. Compare 9 and 29: the speech becomes song and the lure of the nymph's song draws the fisherman down.

4. *cool to his very heart.*

6. *The flood swells up and divides* (as the body emerges from it). Note effect of the inversion —×× —× —.

13. **Fischlein,** dative. **Mir ist** = *I feel.*

16. **erst,** *now for the first time.*

19. **wellenatmend.** The word pictures graphically the rise and fall of the sun's image in the waves.

20. **doppelt schöner** = doppelt schön.

22. **Das feuchtverklärte Blau,** *The azure of the sky transfigured in the water.*

30. *Then he was doomed.* Compare the expression: " he is done for."

14. **Erlkönig** is a corruption of **Elbkönig,** i.e., the king of the elves. Notice the difference in the speeches of the three characters: the calm assuaging tone of the father, whose senses seem dead to the supernatural; the luring song of the **Erlkönig,** that changes abruptly to an impetuous demand; the ever increasing terror of the child till its fear is imparted to the father. The child's speech is driven relentlessly forward by terror; notice the effect of the inversion in 22 and 28: —×× —, etc.

19. **führen den nächtlichen Reihn,** *dance the nightly round.*

20. *and rock thee and dance thee and sing thee to sleep.*

28. *Erlking has done me grievous woe.*

15. Suggested by the Staubbach, a cascade near Lauterbrunnen in Switzerland (October 1779). The poem compares human life in its various aspects to a stream. Notice in this connection how the rhythm varies from stanza to stanza.

12. **Wolkenwellen,** *cloudlike waves.*

24. **hin,** *along.*

26. **weiden,** *let graze or feast,* i.e., mirror.

30. **mischt vom Grund aus,** *stirs from the very bottom.*

16. Willing surrender, contented submission to the will of the Highest is the keynote of this poem.

9. *childlike thrills of awe.*

40, 41. **ihres Daseins. Ihres** refers to **Geschlechter.** To make it refer to **Götter** (and adopting the variant reading **sie** [i.e., **Götter**] instead of **sich**) makes an impossible metaphor, since the picture of a chain with its links cannot describe the eternal and change-less life of the gods, but only human life, generation following generation as link on link in a chain. Compare 31, where Goethe has used **Wellen** with the same purport.

17. Although a part of **Faust,** this poem is none the less a confession of Goethe himself. Over eighty years old, the poet surveys life as a watchman from his high tower, lets his gaze once more wander over the world, when evening comes, and lo, all is good.

11, 12. *And as all things have pleased me, I am pleased with myself,* i.e., the sum total of my life is good.

SCHILLER

Friedrich Schiller was born in Marbach, Württemberg, No-vember 10, 1759. His short life was one great heroic struggle. His first inclination was to study for the ministry, but the rigorous and arbitrary discipline of the Duke Karl Eugen, whose school the boy as the son of an officer had to enter, considered neither aptitude nor desire, and thus Schiller had to study medi-cine and become an army surgeon. That he might shape his own destiny he fled from Württemberg in 1782. The following years, in which Schiller gradually gained the recognition he deserved, were a bitter battle against poverty; and when in 1789 he had been made professor of history in Jena, only two years passed before illness forced him to resign. At that moment generous friends came to his aid, and from now on Schiller could live for his ideals.

As he had mastered the field of history, he now for years put his entire energy into the study of philosophy to round out his Weltanſchauung (his view of life) and his personality. Even as he worked, he knew that his years were numbered, but his indomitable will forced the weak body to do its bidding, and the best of Schiller's dramas, the greatest of his philosophical poems, were written in these years of illness. Thus Schiller proved himself the master of his fate, the captain of his soul. Only a few weeks before his death he wrote to Wilhelm von Humboldt, „Am Ende ſind wir doch beide Idealiſten und würden uns ſchämen, uns nachſagen zu laſſen, daß die Dinge uns formten und wir nicht die Dinge." ("After all both of us are idealists and would be ashamed to have it reported of us that the things fashioned us and not we the things.") There was in Schiller, as Goethe said, ein Zug nach dem Höheren, a trend toward higher things. Schiller died in Weimar, May 9, 1805.

As a poet Schiller is in many respects the exact counterpart of Goethe. The latter's lyric verse is the direct result of his everyday experience; his real domain is the simple lyric, das Lied. Schiller, however, confessed that lyric poetry in the narrower sense was not his province, but his exile. Hardly ever did an everyday experience move him to song, and he is at his best in the realm of philosophic poetry, where he has no equal. This philosophic tendency predominates even in his ballads, which are often the embodiment of a philosophical or ethical idea. While they lack the subtle lyrical atmosphere of Goethe's, they are distinguished by rhetorical vigor and dramatic life. Their very structure is dramatic, as an analysis of **18** and **19** will show.

18. Ibykus, a Greek lyric poet of the sixth century B.C., born in Rhegium, a city in Southern Italy.

1. The Isthmian Games were celebrated every two years on the Isthmus of Corinth in honor of Poseidon (Neptune), god of the sea.

6. Apollo, the god of song, archery and the sun (hence also called Helios, 71).

10. Akrokorinth, the citadel of Corinth, situated on a mountain above the city.

11. The pine was sacred to Poseidon. A wreath of pine was the award of victory in the games (54).

23. **der Gaſtliche.** Zeus, to whom hospitality was sacred.

61. **Prytane,** *m.* –en, prytanis, the chief magistrate.

82. **Bühne,** here used for the tiers of seats for the spectators. Compare Schaugerüſte, 95.

91. **Kekrops' Stadt** = Athens. Kekrops, the legendary founder of the state of Athens. **Aulis,** a harbor in Boeotia.

92. **Phokis,** territory in Greece to the west of Boeotia.

103. **Rieſenmaß.** Since the Greek actors wore buskins and a long mask, the gigantic stature of the chorus is in itself no indubitable proof of the supernatural origin of this chorus. Thus the spectators are unable to decide, whether they actually see the Eumenides or only a chorus impersonating them. This is the meaning of 145 and 146. This doubt yields to certainty as the action progresses (170 ff.).

117. *sense beguiling, heart deluding.*

118. **Erinnyen** or **Eumeniden,** *Eumenides,* are the avenging goddesses of Greek mythology, the Furies.

150. *weaves the dark entangled net of fate.*

173. **gerochen,** common form is gerächt.

182. **die Szene** = Greek σκηνή, *the stage.*

19. The problem of the limitation of human knowledge and of the human mind, already touched upon in Genesis 2, 17, had been brought into prominence in Schiller's time by the philosopher Kant. He had defined the limitations of the human mind: we can have no real knowledge of things themselves, but can know only the impressions that things make on our senses; furthermore our knowledge is limited to the finite, we have no knowledge of the Infinite, the Absolute. Schiller, not satisfied with the mere fact, in this poem expresses the conviction that there must be an ethical reason for this necessity, a reason that is beyond our ken. Compare also the beautiful words of Lessing: ,, Nicht die Wahrheit, in deren Beſitz irgend ein Menſch iſt, oder zu ſein vermeinet, ſondern die aufrichtige Mühe, die er angewandt hat, hinter die Wahrheit zu kommen, macht den Wert des Menſchen. Denn nicht durch den Beſitz, ſondern durch die Nachforſchung der Wahrheit erweitern ſich ſeine Kräfte, worin allein ſeine immer wachſende Vollkommenheit beſtehet. Der Beſitz macht ruhig, träge, ſtolz.

Wenn Gott in seiner Rechten alle Wahrheit, und in seiner Linken den einzigen immer regen Trieb nach Wahrheit, obschon mit dem Zusatze, mich immer und ewig zu irren, verschlossen hielte, und spräche zu mir: wähle! Ich fiele ihm mit Demut in seine Linke und sagte: Vater, gib! die reine Wahrheit ist ja doch nur für dich allein! "

Sais, city in ancient Egypt, seat of a famous shrine to Isis. Ägyptenland, Ägypten = Egypt.

6. Hierophant, ἱεροφάντης (*literally*, the interpreter of the holy), *hierophant*, a priest, the teacher of religious mysteries.

61. *a thrill of heat and cold surges through his frame.*

64. In seinem Innern, *in his heart* or *within him.*

65. den Allheiligen, *the most holy* (*God*). All here has an intensifying meaning.

81. War dahin, *was gone.*

UHLAND

Ludwig Uhland was born April 26, 1787, in Tübingen, where his father and both his grandfathers had been connected with the University. Uhland took up the profession of law, but his heart's desire led him to the study of the older German poetry and folklore, and from 1830 to 1832 he occupied the chair of German Literature in Tübingen. He also took an active part in the political life of his time in the interest of liberal tendencies and a united Germany. He died in Tübingen, November 13, 1862. His poetry is for the most part a product of his earlier years. Reserved and retiring to a fault, Uhland in his lyrics but rarely gives us directly his own emotional life, preferring to let the shepherd, the soldier, the mountain lad speak. The type of the simple folksong predominates, and from the Volkslied Uhland introduced into modern verse the modified Nibelungen stanza and the rhymed couplet. In his ballads Uhland prefers older historical subjects, as in Taillefer, that rarest jewel among his ballads; or at least uses an historic setting, as in the more popular Des Sängers Fluch.

21. — 6. Mutterhaus, i.e., source.
18. rufe zu, *call to them.*

22. Notice how the first line, giving the situation, is repeated at the close of the poem and thus frames the picture.

6. *Sweet thrills of awe, mysterious stirring.*

23. — 12. einmal, *sometime.*

24. — 7. sich ins Feld machen, *to start out into the field.* Compare sich auf den Weg machen, *to start out.*

25. — 67. mit jedem Tag, compare English, *with every passing day.*

27. — 3. in freier Hand, *with free,* i.e., *unsupported, hand.*

4. erfand = fand.

8. soll geholfen sein, *it shall be remedied.*

29. — 1. zogen . . . wohl, render *did journey.*

2. bei, *at the house of;* bei einer Frau Wirtin, *at the inn of mine hostess.*

3. hat Sie, third person singular as formal direct address (obsolete).

13. deckte den Schleier zu, *covered her face with the veil.*

14. dazu, *while doing this.*

17. hub, archaic for hob.

18. an, archaic for auf.

30.— 2. nit, dialectal for nicht.

5. in gleichem Schritt und Tritt, *keeping step.*

6. kam geflogen, *came flying;* kommen is construed with the past participle.

8. Impersonal construction best rendered by the passive.

31. Taillefer, i.e., *iron cutter.*

Duke William of Normandy defeated the English under Harold at Hastings in 1066.

6. schwingt = *turns.* The water was pulled up by a windlass.

14. dabei, *while doing it.*

16. klingen mit Schild und mit Schwert, *make shield and sword rssound.*

25. fuhr wohl, *did journey.*

27. Told by the chronicles. To stumble was an ill omen.

29. zum Sturme schritt, *went to attack.*

35. so läßt mich das entgelten, etc., *let me receive my dues for that,* etc.

40. Roland, one of the famous paladins of Charlemagne; his deeds were much celebrated in song. Held, usually weak.

43. von, render *with.*

45. sprengt' er hinein, i.e., in den Feind. Stoß, *thrust* (of the spear).

47. Schlag, blow (of the sword).

58. in Lieb und in Leid, *in joy and in sorrow.*

32. — 5. reich an, *rich in.*

7. blicken used transitively.

10. grau von Haar. Compare *blue of eyes and fair of hair.*

35. blitzend, *like a flash of lightning.*

42. aller Harfen Preis, *the best of all harps.*

63. Heldenbuch, a book telling of heroes and their deeds.

EICHENDORFF

Joseph Freiherr von Eichendorff, the scion of an old aristocratic family, was born in his ancestral castle in Silesia, March 10, 1788, and died November 26, 1856. Three things especially have left an impression on his poetry: his deeply loved Silesian home with its castle-crowned wooded hills and its beautiful valleys and streams; a simple childlike piety; and an early acquaintance with the Volksbücher and the Volkslied. The only things in Eichendorff's life that have a romantic glamor are his happy, carefree student days and his participation in the Wars of Liberation (1813–1815). When peace was declared, the poet entered the service of the Prussian state and proved himself a careful and trusted official. Thus, living a busy life, he could write that classic of romantic idleness: Aus dem Leben eines Taugenichts, *The Autobiography of a Good-for-Nothing.*

Eichendorff's lyric verse can be described best by Nietzsche's definition of a Lied: ,,Takt als Anfang, Reim als Ende, und als Seele stets Musik.'' Music is the very soul of his lyrics to an unusual

degree. A melody of haunting sweetness dwells in his simple
lines. It is as if the music of Robert Schumann had sought to
clothe itself in words. Coupled with this, we meet a most delicate perception of nature and a remarkable ability to portray her
various aspects and her ever varying moods. Romantic Sehnsucht
(yearning), romantic Wanderlust and the romantic love of nature
have found in Eichendorff their finest expression.

33. — 10. vor, *on account of, because of.*

11. was, *why.*

12. *with free throat and joyous breast.*

16. aufs best', *in the best way.*

34. — 3. wohl, *indeed.*

13. Banner, usually neuter.

16. The forest is the scene of many of the old legends.

21. *Always remain steadfast and true.* Compare: Wir bleiben
die Alten, i.e., our feeling toward each other will not change, we
shall remain true friends.

35. Besides its love of nature and its religious note, both apparent in the previous poems, notice especially the touch of symbolism; the poet stands in Waldesschatten wie an des Lebens
Rand.

5, 6. schlagen herein, *the tones of the bells come pealing into the
shadow of the forest.*

10. von, *down from, on.*

36. This poem describes, as the title indicates, the dawn of
spring: how spring in a moonlight night imparts a mysterious
stirring of new life to all nature. With its variously interwoven
rhymes, both end and internal, its use of assonance and alliteration, to mention only the more obvious effects, the poem is a
musical symphony.

8. Wolkenfrau'n, clouds personified.

11. Frühlingsgesellen, i.e., Waldquellen as helpers of spring.

37. Might well be compared to the elfin dances of Moritz
von Schwind, the romantic painter.

38. — 2. ein Schuß fällt, *a shot (of a gun) is heard.*

40. — 5. entbrennte for entbrannte.

42. Compare with **38**, as to the use of the human element.
1. der Nebel fällt, i.e., sinks away.
2. wie bald sich's rühret, *how soon life will stir.*

43. — 4. Note the onomatopoetic effect of the rhythm.

44. This poem is the quintessence of Eichendorff's lyric verse. Note the construction of the stanzas. The first stanza is composed of two syntactic units: 1 and 2, 3 and 4; the second of four units; notice the effect of the two heavy syllables sternflar; the third stanza reverts in structure to the first. Notice the effect of the inversion in 10: Weit ihre Flügel aus, — × × — × —.

RÜCKERT

Friedrich Rückert, born May 16, 1788, died January 31, 1866, represents the combination of poet and scholar in a more striking degree than even Uhland, but he lacks the latter's rare critical ability regarding his own verse. Oriental languages were his special field, and a most astounding technical skill enabled him to reproduce in German the complex Oriental verse forms with their intricate rhyme schemes. Something of this technical skill is apparent in **45**, the one well-nigh perfect poem of Rückert. The third stanza is an adaptation from a children's rhyme. This the poet uses as the main motif at regular intervals, slightly varying it in the sixth to express his own feelings directly, and closing the poem with it in the ninth. A similar parallelism is apparent in the odd lines of each stanza. The last line of each stanza must be read with three accents: Was mein einst war, × — — —.

45. — 7. ob, I *wonder whether.*

14. Unbewußter Weisheit froh, *joyous in unconscious wisdom,* i.e., full of wisdom and not aware of it.

16. Salomo, *Solomon,* the wise king of the Hebrews. Oriental legends attributed to him magic and supernatural knowledge.

25. wohl, concessive, *it is true.*

HEINE

Heinrich Heine was born in Düsseldorf, December 13, 1797, of Jewish parents. The Napoleonic Wars were among the chief impressions of his childhood. He saw Napoleon ride through Düsseldorf; he saw the tattered remains of the Grande Armée return from the disastrous Russian campaign; and although not without the patriotic fervor of the German youth, he could not but admire the genius of the great Corsican (46). At Hamburg the young Heine was to enter upon a commercial career under the guidance of his rich uncle, but failed. An unrequited love for his cousin Amalie Heine became for a number of years the subject of his song. His favorite, almost exclusive vehicle; of expression is the simple stanza of the Volkslied, which he uses with consummate skill for new effects. Heine's attempts in law proved as futile as those in business; although he did pass his examination for the degree of *Doctor juris*, the study of poetry had been his chief endeavor in his university career. Finally he decided to make literature his profession. Disgruntled with things in general and more especially with Germany — he had been crossed in his love for Amalie's younger sister Therese, the rich uncle not wanting a penniless poet for a son-in-law — Heine went to Paris in 1831, where he lived till his death (February 17, 1856), often reviling but always cherishing and loving Germany, the country of sweet romantic song. Compare his poem In der Fremde (64).

46. The theme of the poem is the loyalty of the humble soldier to his chosen hero. Its tone is utterly realistic, its language and metaphors those of everyday prose. Notice the effects Heine achieves by varying the number of unaccented syllables, e.g., 13 and 33, × — ×—× —× — and × —×× —×× —×× —.

2. waren gefangen, *had been captives.*

6. verloren gehen, *to be lost.*

10. wohl, *indeed;* ob, *because of.*

11. Mir ist weh, *I am sore at heart;* mir wird weh?

13. Das Lied ist aus, *the jig is up, all is over.*

18. Ich trage, *I bear, I cherish.*

47—58. A rearrangement from two cycles, Lyrisches Inter-
mezzo and Heimkehr. The main theme is the poet's unrequited
love for his cousin Amalie Heine (**49**, Therese).

48. The Lorelei is the name of a high cliff overlooking the
Rhine. Clemens Brentano invented the myth, and the theme
became popular in the early decades of the nineteenth century.
Heine gave it its final form, in which it has practically become
a folksong. The first four lines give us the mood of the poet,
the second four give the setting of the action. 9–22 describe
the action. Notice the utter simplicity of 21 and 22, which
characterizes also the short epilogue, 23 and 24. This simple
way of ending a poem Heine has in common with the folksong.

4. *That does not leave my thought.*

18. Impersonal, best rendered by the passive.

50. Notice that this poem has the same tripartite structure
as the preceding. (Heine's decided preference for this structure is evinced by the great number of poems of three stanzas.)

3. Ganges, river in India.

9. This bit of nature description, although unconventional,
does not lack truth. Goethe offers a similar example, when
he speaks of schalkhafte (roguish, waggish) Veilchen.

51. One of the finest of Heine's nature poems.

52. — 6. Morgenland, see Vocabulary.

53. — 8. Nebeltanz, *the dance of the mists.*

54. Notice the realism of tone, not a word that rises above the
plane of everyday prose. A whole tragedy compressed into three
stanzas.

6, 7. *The first man that happened to come her way.*

8. ist übel dran, *is in a sad fix.*

55. Compare **42**, where the Stimmung, the mood, of a bit of
nature is expressed without any reference to any human element. In this poem of Heine the charm of the evening is em-
bodied in the fair nymph. Compare **37**. The same tendency is
apparent in many of the paintings of Schwind and Böcklin.

56. Stanzas 1–3 are each divided into two equal parts. In the third stanza, however, the line of division is less marked; notice also the effect of the inversion in 12: Taucht er ins Fluten-grab, —×× —× —. In the fourth stanza each line stands by itself.

57. Notice the effect of the rhyme combining the first and fourth lines of each stanza. The first two lines of each stanza have four accents, the last two, three. Notice how the metrical structure of the line is made subservient to the mood expressed; this is especially true of 3: Es dunkelt schon, mich schläfert, ×—×— | | ×—×.

59. An apotheosis of Christ, who is represented as the spirit of universal love permeating all things.

17. Sonnenherz, *sun heart*, since the sun is his heart.

22 ff. These lines imitate clearly the pealing of church bells.

36. schauernd in, *thrilled with*.

60. Notice the dainty effect of the tone coloring, heightened by the skilful use of impure rhymes.

61. The charm of this poem, as of many of Heine's, lies in its suggestive power. The course of events is only dimly sketched, the tragic end hardly more than alluded to. While the first two stanzas are composed of two equal parts each, the last is composed of four.

62. — 2, 4. Wohl, translate: *They do*, etc.

63. Of Heine's poems this was the favorite of Lenau. Absolute unity of form and content: ceaseless change in ceaseless monotony.

7. Wo sind sie hin? *Whither are they gone?*

64. — 5. Das, without any definite antecedent.

65. Perhaps the most beautiful poem of Heine's later years. A short ballad has been shaped into a lyric of exquisite simplicity and harmonious restraint. The Asra are a legendary Arabian tribe, passionate and sensitive. Love and death, Eros and Thanatos, seem interdependent.

PLATEN

August Graf von Platen-Hallermünde was born in Ansbach, Bavaria, October 24, 1796, and died near Syracuse, Sicily, December 5, 1835. The son of a noble family, Platen is, barring his Weltschmerz (*world weariness,* compare Lenau) and the fact that he spent a good part of his life in foreign lands, the exact opposite of Heine. While Heine affects a certain carelessness of rhyme and rhythm and diction, Platen observes a studied elegance. His verse form is faultless as if chiselled in marble, his rhymes the most careful and pure. His ballads have a stately majesty of rhythm that reflects the inherent nobility of the poet. On the whole, his stanzas are characterized by a full and sonorous ring, although effects of delicate grace are not wanting (**67**). Platen is one of the greatest masters of form in German literature and is unrivalled as a master of the sonnet.

66. Alarich (*Alaric*), the great leader of the Goths, having conquered Rome, succumbed to a fever when 34 years old (410 A.D.), and was buried by his troops near Cosenza (Cosentia) in the river Busento. Notice the stately dignity of the long trochaic line without any marked caesural pause. Any attempt to introduce the latter spoils the majestic ring of the verse.

1. lispeln, best rendered, *are lisped,* or *resound faintly.*

7. *vied with each other for places in the rows along the stream.*

67. The lily swaying to and fro in the water is perfectly pictured by the rhythm, especially by the recurring five-syllable rhymes.

68. The peculiar effect is largely due to the preponderance of rhymes on a or o which have proved an insurmountable obstacle for every translator. Even Longfellow failed. His rhymes of light, night, change the whole effect.

9. in acht nehmen, *to watch,* in poetry is often construed with the genitive.

14. Refers to the harmony of the spheres.

18. *Deceptively remote distance.*

20. aufs neue, *anew.*

69. Pindar, the greatest of the Greek lyric poets, died according to legend as here described. He is justly famous for his majestic odes, and Platen revered him as his master.

9. Schauspiel, here *theater*.

11. It was customary in Greece for an older man to cultivate the friendship of a youth, e.g., Socrates and Alcibiades.

12. In the Greek drama the action was interspersed with choral odes, which were sung to the accompaniment of flutes.

LENAU

Nikolaus Niembsch von Strehlenau, known as Nikolaus Lenau, the third in the group of the poets of Weltschmerz (Lord Byron is the best example in England), was born in Southern Hungary August 13, 1802. The father, a gambler and libertine, died before the boy was five years old; the mother, a high strung, passionate woman, battled with poverty for the sake of her children, of whom Nikolaus was her idol. His first impression of nature was the silent solitude and vastness of the Hungarian plains, which probably helped to accentuate an inherent strain of melancholy. Led astray by a youthful errant passion, he is haunted by a feeling of guilt, of lost innocence, and Dame Melancholy becomes his faithful life companion. When later happiness in the guise of human love crosses his pathway, he does not dare stretch out his hand. Shuddering, he feels there is something " too fatally abnormal about him that he should affix that heavenly rose to his dark gloomy heart." Living only for his art and ever eager to enrich it with new impressions, he goes to America. There Nature was virgin still, untouched by the hands of man. What a lure! Incidentally he hopes to be cured of his melancholy and to gain an easy competence by investing in government land. After a winter spent on the American frontier (1832–1833) he returns to Germany a sadder, if not a wiser man, and becomes a restless wanderer until in 1844 the fate that he always dreaded overtakes him: his spirit is enshrouded in insanity. Six years later, August 22, 1850, he dies in an asylum near Vienna.

Lenau's poetry is for the most part an expression of intense melancholy, full of " sadness at the doubtful doom of humankind." It abounds in subtle nature descriptions, often quite impressionistic in their effect (**76** and especially **77**). Sometimes the poet employs a homely realism (**75**). Lenau was a master of the violin, and his verse is full of striking rhythmical effects; on the whole he prefers the slower cadences so well suited to his nature.

70. An apostrophe to the night, which is addressed as bu bunfleš Auge.

5, 6. von hinnen nehmen, *to take away.*

8. für und für, *forever and ever.*

71. — 3. Describes vividly the effect of the pale moonlight on the green sedge.

72. — 7. waš for etwaš.

10. will, *wills.*

73. — 1 ff. In German, May is the incarnation of all springtime beauty and bliss. Compare **2** and **110** and the word Maienglück in 29.

3. ob = über.

8. Straßen, old weak dative.

12. Frühlingšfinder, i.e., birds.

29 f. mitten in . . . innen, *in the midst of.*

42. mag, *may.*

44. Erden, see note on 8.

46. 'š ift ewig ſchade, *it is too bad, it is a pity.*

56. dränge, subjunctive of purpose.

59. ob, instead of alš ob. Common with Lenau.

60. ſtimmen, instead of einſtimmen; in ein Lied einſtimmen = *to join in a song.*

63. lag, *lingered.*

74. The heavy, slow moving rhythm is in apt harmony with the scene portrayed.

12. einer um den andern, *one after another, in turn.*

75. — 13. daš aufgeſchlagne Gebet, *the prayer to which the book was opened.*

76. This may be the direct description either of a Dutch landscape or of a painting. Holland, like most of the North Sea Plain, is one vast level expanse of country, through which the rivers and brooks move but sluggishly. Here and there a Dutch windmill looms up; like all other objects it seems to peer forth from a haze because of the moisture-laden atmosphere. Nowhere else does nature assume such a bewitchingly drowsy aspect in autumn as here.

10. ob, compare note to **73**, 59. trutze = trotze.

11. Strohkapuze, refers to the straw thatched roof.

77. — 6. in eins fallen, *to coalesce.*

8. *And in sadness become oblivious of each other.*

9. hin und wieder, *back and forth.*

78. The last of Lenau's Waldlieder. The morbid melancholy of the poet has softened, and death is to him heimlich still vergnügtes Tauschen, *silent sweet passing from one state to another.*

5. von hinnen, *away.*

MÖRIKE

Eduard Mörike was born in Ludwigsburg, September 8 1804. Circumstances forced him into the study of theology, and so ne passed through the schools preparatory to the famous Tübingen School of Divinity, where he completed his studies. He proved but an indifferent student (his thorough knowledge of Greek and Latin was in good part the result of later studies), he preferred to live in a fairy world of his own creation. Nature, music, and poetry were his delight, and of all the poets Goethe was always his favorite. For eight years Mörike was curate in various villages of Württemberg, more than once tempted to give up the ministry, but finally realizing that there was no better place to live his poet dreams than the attic room of a Suabian parsonage.

In 1834 he became pastor in Cleversulzbach, a secluded little village, nestling among the Suabian hills. Here the poet, with his mother and sister, lived an idyllic existence, his most frequent visitor the Muse. Ill health forced him to resign in 1843. and Mörike once more became a wanderer. During these years love again crossed his path, and to be able to marry — his pension was too meager — he accepted (1851) a position at a girls' seminary in Stuttgart, where he taught German Literature for one or two hours a week, a none too heavy and an altogether congenial task. Mörike died June 4, 1875.

Mörike's poetry gives abundant proof of a rich creative imagination. Even his everyday speech was of an astounding concreteness, and thus the various aspects of Nature assume bodily shape. Spring becomes a youth, the symphony of spring the soft tone of a harp (**81**); the night — a fairy woman — leans against the rocky cliff listening to the azure of the sky (**79**). Although the idyllic predominates, deeper tragic notes are not wanting (**84, 85**) nor is the full note of exuberant joy (**86**). But early in life Mörike realized that any overflowing measure of joy or grief would prove destructive to his oversensitive nature, and the golden mean became inevitably his ideal (**88**). Never has he expressed that sweet serenity of soul, which he gained not without a bitter struggle, more beautifully than in the melodious lines: „Auf eine Lampe" (**87**).

79. In its allegorical personification the poem might be compared to a painting of Böcklin. Like Venus of yore, the night rises from the sea and at midnight sees the golden balance of time (the heavenly bodies) rest in equilibrium. The springs try to lull the night, their mother, to sleep with a song of the beauty of the day. She prefers the azure melody of the midnight sky, but the waters continue to sing, even in their sleep, of the day that has just passed. This contest the poet also portrays rhythmically: compare the measured trochaic movement of the first half of each stanza with the lighter dactylic movement of the second half. (Each line begins with an Auftakt.)

5. **fecfer**, since the noises of the day no longer interfere with their song.

12. In apposition with des Himmels Bläue. The firmament is the yoke along which the fleeting hours glide; **gleichgeschwungen,** *equally arched*, i.e., perfectly circular.

80. — 3. Schleier, of mist.

5. **Herbstkräftig**, full of autumnal vigor; **gedämpft,** because the

mists and the haze have softened all sharpness of outline and color.

81. — 1. blaues Band, metaphorical for blue sky.

7. Harfenton, the symphony of spring, the heard and un-heard stirring of new life.

82. The stanza form is an adaptation of a famous Lutheran hymn: Wie schön leuchtet der Morgenstern.

83. Of the character of the Feuerreiter, a creation of Mörike, only this much is clear: he fights fire and has often used sinfully (freventlich) holy means (des heil'gen Kreuzes Span) to charm fire. Finally, however, he becomes a victim of the infernal powers.

21. der rote Hahn, the symbol of fire.

26. Feind, Satan.

40. As the refrain in the preceding stanzas has depicted the tolling of the bell, so the sudden break here depicts the ceasing.

42. Mützen, old weak dative.

84. In its beautiful simplicity this song has become a folksong. Since it presents many metrical irregularities, the following scansion may be found useful. A dot is used to indicate pitch accent.

```
×̇— × —× —           —×× —× —
×× —×× —×           —×× —×
×̇—× — ×—           × —× —× —
× —× —×             × —× —×

×̇—× —× —           —×× —× —
× —×× —×            —×× —×
× —× — —            × —× —× —
× —× —×             × —× —×
```

86. Mörike found the name Rohtraut by chance in an old German lexicon. The full vowel coloring appealed to him and called forth this ballad.

5. Tut etc., dialectic periphrastic conjugation = fischt und jagt.

19. wunniglich (wonniglich). 22. vergunnt (vergönnt) — these archaic forms are in keeping with the tone of the ballad and the patriarchal life at King Ringang's court.

87. Appropriately written in the stately Greek trimeter (iambic verse of six feet). Compare with this poem the closing lines of Keats' *Ode to a Grecian Urn:*

> Beauty is truth, truth beauty, that is all
> Ye know on earth and all ye need to know.

Was aber ſchön iſt, ſelig ſcheint es in ihm ſelbſt.
But beauty seems a thing all blessed within itself.

6. ſchlingt den Ringelreihn, *circle about in a round dance.*
10. ihm, old reflexive instead of ſich.

88. The confession of Mörike's ideal.

1. willt = willſt.

2. *A thing of joy or a thing of sorrow.*

5–7. wolleſt nicht überſchütten, *pray do not overwhelm with a flood of.*

89. Lines of three and of two accents alternate, so that the poem is really written in blank verse; its character is, however, entirely changed, since the last word of each line stands out because of the necessary rhythmical pause. Notice the change in the last two lines.

HEBBEL

Friedrich Hebbel, Germany's greatest master of tragedy since the days of Schiller, was born March 18, 1813, in the little village of Wesselburen in Holstein. Thus his first impression of nature was the infinite expanse of the North Sea Plain. Bitterest poverty was his lot from childhood; poverty and loneliness put their harsh imprint on his youth and early manhood. Haunted by hunger, he battled for years to gain a mere living, often on the brink of despair. His only help was a small stipend from the king of Denmark, which enabled him to spend two years in Paris and Rome, and the meager pennies that his devoted friend Elise Lensing, a poor seamstress in Hamburg, sent him. His short stories, his dramas, although they brought him fame, were of little avail in this struggle that seemed all too hopeless. Then a sudden change for the better came. Stopping at Vienna

on his return from Rome, he found himself in a small circle of
ardent admirers. He met Christine Enghaus, at that time
Germany's greatest tragic actress, who became the most congenial
interpreter of Hebbel's heroines. The attraction was mutual,
and on May 26, 1846, Friedrich Hebbel and Christine Enghaus
were married. Now followed years of calm maturity, the greatest period of Hebbel's dramatic production. Hebbel died in
Vienna December 13, 1863. His lyric poetry, for the most
part the product of his earlier years, is marked above all by a
tendency towards symbolism, these symbols usually of a rich
sensuous beauty and often of a rare delicacy. A homely realism
is, however, by no means lacking. The musical quality of his
verse attracted the genius of Robert Schumann, who set the
Nachtlied to music.

90. In the spring of 1836 Hebbel went to Heidelberg. A child
of the North Sea Plain, he came in contact here with a richer,
softer beauty of a more Southern landscape, a beauty which seemed
to set free his latent powers. A night in the month of May on
the wooded summits near Heidelberg called forth this song. The
giant magnitude of the starry heavens awakened in the poet to
an overpowering degree the feeling of the greatness of cosmic
life; he feels the insignificance of his own individual existence, he feels as if it were in danger of being extinguished by
the vastness of the great All; but then sleep comes as a kindly
nurse and draws her protecting circle about the meager flame
of individual existence. Notice the internal rhymes in the
first and second stanzas that picture cosmic life and its reflection in the individual, and the utterly different effect of the third
stanza, that depicts the narrower sphere of individual life.

91. — 3. spielt herein, *comes playing into the room.*
6. gefällt ihm gar zu sehr, *it likes all too well.*

92. — 10. It was customary for the neighbors to perform the
last kindly offices for the dead.
16. was, *which.*

93. — 1. Die du, *thou who.*

95. — 6 ff. **Wir sterben:** because in this union, when even the last barrier separating the "I" from the "Thou" has fallen, the aim of life has been reached in utter harmony which overcomes the limitations of individual existence. Thus these two souls may return into the All, as expressed in the beautiful symbol of the last stanza.

11. **zerfließen in eins,** *coalesce.*

97. Compare Keats' *Ode to Autumn.*

KELLER

Gottfried Keller, best known as the master of the *Novelle*, was born in Zürich, July 19, 1819, as the son of a master turner. A love for the concrete world of reality induced him to take up painting. Keller was not without talent in this line, but achieving no signal success, he gave up painting for letters. To secure for himself a stable footing in the civic world, Keller, after a number of years spent in Germany, in 1861 assumed the office of secretary of his native canton. He died in Zürich, July 15, 1890. Early in life, Keller threw aside all conventional beliefs, and his religion henceforth was a deep love of and a joyous faith in all life. Although Keller was in many respects decidedly matter-of-fact, a calm objective observer with a strong leaning toward utilitarian ideals — he had all the homely virtues of his ancestry — he nevertheless delighted in a myth-creating fancy. Thus Keller is very much akin to his countryman Arnold Böcklin, whom the German world honors as its greatest modern painter.

98. One of the finest expressions extant of love for one's native land. The various national anthems pale before its beauty.

3. **ob** = obgleich.

9. **Helvetia,** *Switzerland.*

13. **Gut und Hab** (usually **Hab und Gut**), *possessions;* render, *all that I have.*

15. **ob,** compare 3.

99. The grief and woe of Nature held by the fetters of winter personified by this nymph climbing the „Seebaum," whose

branches are held by the ice. A mythical creation such as
Böcklin delighted in.

12. **Glied um Glied,** *limb upon limb,* i.e., *each separate limb.*

14. **her und hin,** *forth and back.*

16. The very sound of this line is a cry of pity.

100. Written 1879. Theodor Storm called it the best lyric
poem since Goethe. Compare C. F. Meyer's letter to Keller
congratulating him on his seventieth birthday. Meyer praises
Keller's poetry because of its „innere Heiterkeit,“ and continues:
„Auch meine ich, daß Ihr fester Glaube an die Güte des Daseins die
höchste Bedeutung Ihrer Schriften ist. Ihnen ist wahrhaftig nichts
zu wünschen als die Beharrung in Ihrem Wesen. Weil Sie die Erde
lieben, wird die Erde Sie auch so lange als möglich festhalten.“

STORM

Theodor Storm, like Friedrich Hebbel, is a child of the North
Sea Plain; but while in Hebbel's verse there is hardly any direct
reference to his native landscape, Storm again and again sings
its chaste beauty; and while Hebbel could find a home away
from his native heath, Storm clung to it with a jealous love.
He was born in Husum (die graue Stadt am grauen Meer) on
the west coast of Schleswig-Holstein, September 14, 1817,
of well-to-do parents. While still a student of law, he published
a first volume of verse together with Tycho and Theodor Momm-
sen. His favorite poets were Eichendorff and Mörike, and the
influence of the former is plainly discernible even in Storm's
later verse. Storm left his home in 1851 and did not return until
1864, after Schleswig-Holstein had become German. He died
July 4, 1888.

101. The poem is one of the very few that depict the change
of night and day as the result of the Earth's turning on its axis.
The verdant orb of the Earth swings into the morning dawn.
While Keller praises the night (die Sternenzeit) because it opens
mystic vistas for us, he no less joyously acclaims the coming of
the new day. His jubilating prayers are evoked as much by
the rising sun as by the Sternenzeit to which he bids farewell.

Storm is the poet of the North Sea Plain: he discovered its peculiar beauty. While the tragic note predominates, joy and humor nevertheless abound, and at the beginning of his poems Storm himself significantly placed his Oftoberlied, written in the political gloom and uncertainty of the fall of 1848. While realizing fully its inherent tragic elements, Storm loved and glorified life and thirstily drank in its beauty to the very last. This is the keynote of Storm's lyrics.

102. — 21. die blauen Tage, *azure days*, i.e., *days blue as the heavens in June.*

103. — 6. *my heart is filled with joyous fright.*

104. — 2. Stein, i.e., *millstone.*
8. Puf, *Puck*, an elfin spirit of mischief. Compare Shakspere, *Midsummer Night's Dream.*

105. The poet's tribute to his home city Husum, „die graue Stadt am grauen Meer."
13. für und für, *forever and ever.*

107. In memory of the poet's sister.
8. recht Geschwister, *true brother and sister.*
11 f. Noch weht ein Kinderfrieden mich an, *still a breath of child-hood peace comes to me.*

108. — 18. Pfingstglocken; Pfingsten, *Pentecost*, is celebrated as a summer festival. In Northern Germany house doors are wreathed with birch twigs, while young birch trees are placed upright on the wings of the numerous windmills.

109. — 6. Mir ist, etc., *I feel (full of life) like*, etc.

110. — 1. vivat, Latin, *long may he live*, render *hurrah!*

111. — 8. *what otherwise would be honorable.*

112. Storm has used the same motif in Immensee.

113. — 7. Schlag, i.e., *pulsation (beat) of pain.*

MEYER

Conrad Ferdinand Meyer was born October 12, 1825, in Zürich, and is thus a fellow-townsman of Keller. Like Keller, Meyer is a master of the *Novelle*, but in all other respects there is a most striking difference. Keller was a sturdy commoner and always retained a certain affinity with the soil; there is a wholesome vigor about him. Meyer is of patrician descent; his father, who died early, was a statesman and historian; his mother a highly gifted woman of fine culture. Thus the boy grew up in an atmosphere of refinement. Having finished the Gymnasium, he took up the study of law, but history and the humanities were of greater interest to him. Even in the child two traits were observed that later characterized the man and the poet: he had a most scrupulous regard for neatness and cleanliness, and he lived and experienced more deeply in memory than in the immediate present. Meyer found himself only late in life; for many years also, being practically bilingual, he wavered between French and German. The Franco-German War brought the final decision, and from now on his works appeared in rapid succession. He died in his home in Kilchberg above Zürich, November 28, 1898.

Meyer's lyric verse is almost entirely the product of his later years. It has none of the youthful exuberance of Goethe's earlier lyrics; a note of quiet calm, a mellow maturity pervades all; both joy and sorrow live only in the memory. And still Meyer loved life's exuberant fullness, and a more finely attuned ear hears through this calm the beat of a heart that felt joy and sorrow deeply. Everywhere there is apparent a love of nature interpreted with all the modern subtlety of feeling. Meyer was a Swiss and his landscape is that of Switzerland, one might even say that of Zürich. Nature hardly ever speaks in herself, but only in her human relationship; not the field alone, but the field and the sower (**121**), the field and the reaper (**118**); not the lake alone, but the lake and the solitary oarsman (**124**). The poet loves the work of human hands and especially its highest form, that of art. Thus a Roman fountain (**119**), a picture, a statue become the subject of his verse. Of all the arts he loved sculpture most, and in its chaste self-restraint his poetry is like

marble. Give marble a voice and you have a poem of Conrad
Ferdinand Meyer. His poetry is also akin to marble in its perfection of form that is faultless, because it is the living rhythmic
embodiment of an idea, of an experience. Witness but the
melody and the rhythm of ber römifdje Brunnen or of the Säer=
fprud. In English letters Walter Savage Landor is a kindred
spirit and his *Finis*, except for a note of haughty pride, might
well be the epitaph of the Swiss poet:

> I strove with none, for none was worth my strife.
> Nature I loved and, next to Nature, Art:
> I warmed both hands before the fire of life;
> It sinks, and I am ready to depart.

114. — 9–14. A series of „Lieberfeefen." Every one of these
lines contains the idea of one of Meyer's poems; compare **116.**
  11. gen . . . empor, *up towards.*

115. — 10. bumpfen Ruberß, a case of transferred epithet.
The sound goes, of course, with Schlagen.

116. — 8. frägt, usually fragt.
  11. Du tuft Dir'ß felbft zu leib, *You do it* (i.e., *stay away*) *to
your own grief.*
  12. Waß für ein, *what kind of a.*

119. The theme of Meyer's lyrics often is a painting, a piece
of sculpture, etc. Here a typical Roman fountain has found
lasting embodiment.
  2. ber Marmorfchale Runb, *the round hollow of the marble basin.*

120. — 3. zum erften, *at first.*

121. The poem in its rhythm embodies the rhythm of the
sower. Compare Millet's painting *The Sower.*

122. — 4. nicht einer, ber barbe, *not one that may suffer want.*

123. The Dutch school of painting is famous for its realism
and its truth to life. The effect of this poem is due in no small

mean to contrast: „das kleine zarte Bild" of the first two lines described, 12 ff., and the „Junfer mit der Dirn, der vor Gesundheit fast die Wange birst"; the quiet of death, the quiet grief of the master, and the boisterous fullness of life.

Nach, *according to, from.*

3. Es pocht, *Somebody knocks.* Herein, *come in.*

5. Vor, *because of.*

6. Von, *with.*

10. zur Stunde, *at once.*

16. nach der Natur, *from life.*

126. It is necessary to bear in mind that in Switzerland dusk first settles in the valleys and then gradually creeps up to the villages situated on a higher level.

8. Kilchberg, the poet's home near Zürich.

128. — 3. Gemahl, *n.* in poetry instead of Gemahlin.

4. Morgenschauer, *the cool morning breezes,* the chill that falls just before sunrise.

12. Sommerhöhn, the higher meadows where the cattle can graze only in the summer months.

LILIENCRON

Detlev von Liliencron, a countryman of Hebbel and Storm, was born in Kiel, June 3, 1844. He loved a soldier's life and served his country in two wars, 1866 and 1870–71, and thus saw life in its grim reality. Because of wounds and debts, he tells us, he left the army. An inborn love of adventure and action made him try his fortune in America, where his mother's father had served under Washington. His aim was to enter the military service of one of the Central or South American states. Disappointed in his hopes, he returned to Germany and for a number of years was a government official. This task, however, proved too irksome for his restless spirit, and in spite of his continual financial embarrassments, he resigned to live as he pleased. He died in Hamburg, July 22, 1909.

In his younger days, Liliencron felt the throb and stir of life far too keenly to find leisure for literature. Not till 1884 did his first volume of verse appear, recollections of his soldier days. The volume contains graphic descriptions of the most concise brevity, single words taking the place of whole sentences (**132**).

He delineates war with all its horror, not however without a sad pathos (**133**). He is also a master at depicting the more joyous side of a soldier's life, the carefree maneuvres of a regiment with its colors and music passing through a village (**130**). In his love of nature Liliencron is akin to Storm, and even surpasses the older poet in the impressionistic vividness of his descriptions.

130. The poem pictures a German village scene: soldiers with their music approach from the distance, march through and disappear.

3. **bricht'ß,** *breaks forth* or *bursts forth.*

6 ff. The attention is first focused on the deeper notes. A gradual rise in pitch is noticeable in the lines from instrument to instrument named.

24. **Laternenglaß,** of the street lanterns.

29. **Wilhel(mine), Katharine (Trine), Chri(stine)**

131. — 9. **firrt,** an onomatopoetic word coined by the poet to imitate the sound of the scythe cutting through the grain.

10. **Arbeitsfrieden,** *the quiet peace of daily labor.*

11. **Heimatwelt,** *home world.* Compare **Alltagswelt,** *work-a-day world.*

132. — 4. *march and flood of victory.*

11 f. **durch die Lüfte braust,** etc., *with horrible whir of wings a flight of vultures passes through the air.*

133. Famous battle in the Seven Years War, in which Frederick the Great was defeated with enormous losses by the Austrians.

2. **Sommerhalm,** lit. summerstalk, i.e., *growing grain.*

4. **ist aus,** *is over.*

9. *he had to go.*

16. **Bevern,** a small town in Brunswick.

22. **hinein,** into the book.

134. — 4. **Winzervolf,** collective sing. Best rendered as plural of **Winzer.**

136. A lullaby for the poet's son 𝔚ulff (*Wolf*).

3. 𝔐onbe𝔰kaḥn, i.e., the crescent moon, shaped like a boat. Render the line, *slowly the crescent moon floats like a boat.*

137. — 5. *The content of life not stirred by a breeze.*

138. — 6 ff. 𝔖onnengrün . . . weiß . . . ſtill. The peculiar effect of sunlight on colors and on quiet is depicted by these compounds.

14. =fältig, *-fold.*

16. *slowly the dusk of evening lowers.*

DEHMEL

Richard Dehmel was born near Berlin, November 18, 1863, and died in Blankenese, a suburb of Hamburg, February 8, 1920. Born twenty years later than his friend Liliencron, he is more directly the child of our modern industrial age. The plight of the laborer, the proletarian, becomes one of his most pressing problems, as the poem 𝔇er 𝔄rbeit𝔰mann shows. But notice that the poet does not depict the 𝔄rbeit𝔰mann in the smoke of the factory or the noisy squalor of the overcrowded tenement, but on Sunday when he has time to be a human being and can walk with his child through the summer fields. The impressionistic vividness of the opening lines of the second stanza recalls Liliencron and — Eichendorff, the most romantic of the Romantic lyrists. Dehmel's birthplace and the home of his childhood was not Berlin, the great metropolis, but a forester's home in the country. Every sense became attuned to the pulsating life in field and forest. A mystic quality arising from a close and intimate perception of everyday reality becomes apparent. While revolutionary turbulence and loud and crass effects sometimes mar his earlier lyrics, in his best poems he soon achieved harmonious clarity. A deeply religious acceptance of life as our most precious gift brings Dehmel close to Goethe and Keller. Compare **17** and **101** with the poems of Dehmel.

139. Notice how the closing words of the first stanza become the Leitmotif, how this increases in intensity until it reaches its climax in the closing line of the poem. We sense the threat of the oncoming social revolution.

9. **Schwalbenvolf.** The swallows are not individual birds or separate pairs as other birds, but they form a collective group that lives and works together.

140. The day ends in foggy darkness that obliterates the moon and the stars, muffles every sound, and hides most buildings from view. Thus the first two stanzas. Now notice the change in the final stanza, its opening **doch**!

141. Compare with **130**. Liliencron gives us a delightful sequence of colorful sense perceptions. In the brief compass of one eight-line stanza Dehmel does vastly more: the sensory perceptions unveil to us the agonized loneliness of a woman waiting in vain for her husband or her son or her lover.

142. Immediately after sunset every object stands revealed with striking clarity against the paling sky. Every line seems accentuated. And in the settling silence all sounds become mysteriously meaningful.

143. The preceding poem should have prepared the reader for this: the day's close as a symbol of life's closing.

4. **drückend ferne.** An expression of utmost weariness: the tired hands seem to have become alien entities.

144. The poet himself has explained the meaning of this poem. A husband is bidding his wife final farewell. Line 14 tells us that for this couple life's purpose has been achieved: they have freed each other from suffering, the suffering that is the inevitable concomitant of loneliness. The soul thus freed can return to its haven where beyond these voices there is peace.

145 and **146**. Dehmel's unqualified and grateful acceptance of life has found its fullest expression in these two poems. In the first of these we see that even suffering is a blessing in disguise if we but drink deep and unafraid from the bourne of life.

5, 6. **Der tiefe Wasserschacht** is the well (life) whose water in the deep darkness below becomes a faithful mirror for him who looks steadily into it.

In the second poem notice how the immediate reality of earth (𝔟𝔯𝔬𝔱𝔴𝔞𝔯𝔪) becomes one with the blue heaven above. Compare this poem with **44**.

7. 𝔟𝔩𝔞𝔲𝔢 𝔍ü𝔫𝔤𝔩𝔦𝔫𝔤𝔰𝔷𝔢𝔦𝔱: blue was the favorite color of the Romantic poets. Youth is the time of sweet and daring dreams, since life's often painful limitations have not as yet obtruded themselves on our consciousness. And this is as it should be.

STEFAN GEORGE

Stefan George was born in Büdesheim near the Rhine, July 12, 1868, and died in Locarno, Switzerland, December 4, 1933. The austere Roman urge to form seems to be the one compelling influence in his life and art. He might well have said with Horace: *Odi profanum vulgus et arceo.* He held himself aloof in both life and letters from all that is vulgar and commonplace. He had his verse printed in a severe archaic type and made it accessible only to a chosen few. The same austere spirit was not only reflected in his handwriting and in his garb, but, as his last portraits show, it had even shaped his features.

The opening lines of poem **147** describe the chaste and cool simplicity of a steel bracelet, the symbol of the poetry he wanted to write. But neither the poet nor his age were ready for this, and therefore chaste simplicity had to yield for a time to exotic exuberance (lines 5–8 of **147**). But the reader can hardly fail to notice the restraint in the content and the style of the following poems. What is loud and exuberant seems banished. In poem **149** joy is experienced only in retrospect, and the autumn landscape furnishes the fitting setting. As spring is the season of ardent hope and summer marks life's exuberant fullness, so autumn is the season of quiet retrospection. Perhaps the easiest approach to George's verse is through poem **150**. It shows that all things here are transitory. We can only accept this, it is idle to rebel: the frailty of all things here (to quote Shelley) is in us. If this insight dims our hopes it also opens a pathway to kindly forbearance and tolerance, to that *caritas generis humani* which the Christian religion seeks to instill. This is the poet's final message as succinctly stated in the two brief stanzas of poem

151. The light from above is not only for a chosen few but for all, and in due time it comes to all. It blesses us even when at the heat of noon it burns us with excessive brightness. And when it leaves us at evening to bless another people, let us be grateful.

Stefan George allows capitals only at the beginning of a line and for proper nouns or for special emphasis. He limits his punctuation to a bare minimum: instead of semicolons and commas he uses a perpendicular hyphen ' to indicate necessary pauses.

148. While the setting is in the time of the Crusades the experience described is universally valid.

151. — 4. wes't. Compare the participle gewefen and the Old English infinitive *wesán*. Wefen is the old infinitive form, but in Modern German there is a sharp difference of meaning between fein and wefen. The latter is not the mere copula: wefen is more vitally meaningful, includes action. Thus the noun Wefen, like the English equivalent *being*, can refer only to living things, never to inanimate objects.

RILKE

No other lyric poet has struck home in our day like Rainer Maria Rilke, not only in Germany, but also in Italy, France, England, and the United States. Rilke does not concern himself with the hero acclaimed on the marketplace, he praises instead the humble and the lowly and sees in the beggar or the child the pivotal center of life. He can praise the thimble as our ultimate ideal because it fulfills its mission so perfectly. Would we not have achieved the millennium here and now if every human being fulfilled his mission as perfectly as the thimble does? No one can overlook the deeply religious significance of this attitude.

Rainer Maria Rilke was born in Prague, December 4, 1875, and died in Vaud, Switzerland, December 29, 1926. Bohemian folksongs, the simple Bohemian peasant, the Gothic architecture of Prague are the most vital memories of his childhood. In Worpswede near Bremen Rilke joined a colony of artists that found beauty in the flat, silent moors of the North German

plains and drew inspiration from the simple piety of the peas-
antry there. In Russia Rilke came under the spell of Tolstoy,
that strange anomaly of a Christian in our modern times.
Rilke was impressed even more deeply by the pious humility
of the Russian peasant. In France Rilke became the friend of
the great sculptor Rodin, who taught him the need of incessant
work and in whose sculpture life was revealed to him as a succession of ever changing surfaces: all is in flux, life is a ceaseless
change (ein ewiges Werden, fein Sein). And in life's eternal
change Rilke himself became a wanderer without a home. Two
books always accompanied him: the works of the Danish poet
novelist Jens Peter Jacobsen, whom the English world has barely
begun to discover, and the Bible. Jacobsen is spiritually closely
akin to Rilke. And why the Bible? Where is there another
book that reveals so fully and vividly life in its fundamental
aspects in unforgettable stories, symbols, and images? The
Bible became a veritable treasure-trove for the poet Rilke.

152. The poet's love for the simple and humble is evident in
his language. He prefers words that other poets seem to have
shunned because of their lowly simplicity. In his verse they
assume new meaning, new life.

153. The panther is stripped of all royal heroic attributes. In
captivity he is only the vessel of his fate. All else has become
a meaningless memory.

154. An everyday human fate and its ready acceptance. A
young woman knows she is losing her eyesight. The poet makes
us see the symptoms of which the other guests seem oblivious.
The closing lines portray her grateful acceptance.

155. Our modern aim seems to be to strip life of every shred
of mystery in favor of full rational comprehension. Why not
accept instead every day with its gifts, as a child stretches out
its eager hands for the petals that drop from the blossoming trees
in June, holding none, but joyously eager for the next? See
the Gospel of Luke, 6, 34.

156. I have added the title because Rilke wrote these lines as a dedication in a copy of his Stunbenbuch. A young woman had sent him her copy. The peculiar slant of the poem becomes apparent in the opening words. While the more conventional view would speak of an ascent to God and a soaring flight, Rilke speaks of an Abstieg, a descent. Only deep humility leads to God, a receptive and obedient attitude that would make the human individual the humbly receptive vessel of His will. Die leeren Krüge stand in telling contrast to bie hingewillten Hände: the latter an apt symbol of our very self as executor of the Divine will, the former mere alien appurtenances of rank or position.

VOCABULARY

As this book presupposes a knowledge of elementary grammar, pronouns, numerals, the common prepositions, and modal and auxiliary verbs are not given. Of strong verbs only the vowel change, including the quantity when different from the infinitive, is indicated, unless the verb shows further irregularities. Intransitive verbs that take fein contrary to rule are marked with f. The prefix of separable verbs is followed by =. Of nouns only the plural is given, unless they belong to the so-called mixed declension. Compound words whose meaning is readily discernible from the component parts are not included.

A

Abend, *m.* –e evening

Abendrot, *n.* evening glow

abends, *adv.* in the evening

Abendschein, *m.* evening light *or* glow

ab=fallen, ie, a; ä, *intr.* fall off

Abglanz, *m.* reflection, reflected light

Abgrund, *m.* ⸗e abyss

ab=kehren, *refl.* turn away

ab=leiten, *tr.* lead aside

ab=lenken, *tr.* turn aside, divert

ab=messen, ā, e; i, *tr.* measure off

ab=nehmen, a, omm; imm, *tr.* take off

ab=reisen, *intr.* leave on a journey

Abschied, *m.* departure, farewell

ab=schmeicheln, *tr.* obtain by flattery

Abstieg, *m.* –e descent

ab=streifen, *tr.* slip off

ab=zählen, *tr.* count off

ach alas, ah

achten, *tr.* heed, care for (*poet. with gen.*)

acht=geben, a, e; i, *intr.* give heed

ächzen, *intr.* groan

Ade, *n.* farewell

Ader, *f.* –n vein, blood vessel

ahnen, *tr. and intr.* divine, have a foreboding of

ahnungsvoll full of sweet foreboding; ominous

Ähre, *f.* –n ear of grain

Ährenfeld, *n.* –er field of ripening grain

All *n.* the universe; entirety, unison

allda there

allerkleinst very smallest

Alltag, *m.* everyday, weekday

allzu, *adv.* (*in compounds*) much too, all too

Alpe, *f.* –n the Alps

alt old

Alter, *n.* — age

Altersschwäche, *f.* senility, weakness of old age

Amme, *f.* –n nurse

Amſelſchlag, *m.* song of the Amsel (*kind of blackbird*)

an=beten, *tr.* worship

Anbetung, *f.* –en worship, adoration

an=blicken, *tr.* look at

an=brechen, ā, o; i, *intr.* dawn; break

an=fangen, i, a; ä, *tr.* begin

an=faſſen, *tr.* catch hold of, seize

an=gehen, ging, gegangen *intr.* be possible

Angel, *m.*, *f.* –ß, –n fishhook

Angeſicht, *n.* –er face, countenance

Angſt, *f.* ᵘᵉ fear, anguish

ängſten, ⎫ *tr.* cause fear, fright-
ängſtigen ⎰ en; *refl.* be afraid

an=halten, ie, a; ä, *tr.* stop; *intr.* last

an=klagen, *tr.* accuse

an=klingen, a, u, *intr.* begin sounding

an=legen, *tr.* put on, don

an=rufen, ie, u, *tr.* implore, call upon

an=ſchauen, *tr.* look at, gaze at

an=ſehen, a, e; ie, *tr.* look at

an=ſpannen, *tr. and intr.* make tense

an=ſtimmen, *tr.* strike up *or* start (*a song*)

an=ſtoßen, ie, o; ö, *tr.* strike, knock against; clink glasses

Antlitz, *n.* –e face, countenance

Antwort, *f.* –en answer

an=vertrauen, *tr.* entrust

an=wehen, *tr.* blow *or* breathe upon

an=wenden, *reg. or* wandte, gewandt, *tr.* use, employ

Apfel, *m.* ᵘ apple

Arbeit, *f.* –en work, labor

Ärger, *m.* vexation, anger

arm poor

Arm, *m.* –e arm

Art, *f.* –en kind, type

Arzt, *m.* ᵘᵉ physician

Aſche, *f.* –n ashes

Aſien Asia

Aſt, *m.* ᵘᵉ branch

Atem, *m.* respiration, breath

atemlos breathless

Atemzug, *m.* ᵘᵉ breath, respiration

Äther, *m.* ether (*i.e.*, the blue heavens)

atmen, *intr. and tr.* breathe

auf=bauen, *tr.* build up, erect

auf=decken, *tr.* uncover, lay bare; raise, lift

auf=donnern, *tr.* dress ostentatiously

Aufenthalt, *m.* –e abode

auf=erziehen, erzog, erzogen, *tr.* bring up, rear

auf=fangen, i, a; ä, *tr.* catch, capture, receive

auf=finden, a, u, *tr.* find, discover

auf=gehen, (*see* gehen) *intr.* rise (*of the sun, moon*); ein Licht= lein geht auf a light begins to shine

auf=hangen, i, a, *tr.* suspend, hang up

auf=heben, o, o, *tr.* pick up, raise

auf=hören, *intr.* stop, cease

auf=raffen, *tr.* snatch up; *refl.* rise quickly

aufrecht upright, erect

auf=reichen, *intr.* reach upward

aufrichtig honest

auf=sammeln, *tr.* gather, collect

auf=schieben, o, o, *tr. and refl.*
"shove open" (*i.e.*, to open)

auf=schlagen, u, a; ä, *tr.* open (*a
book*)

auf=schweben, *intr.* soar up

auf=springen, a, u, *intr.* spring
up, jump up

auf=stehen, stand, gestanden, *intr.*
arise, get up

auf=steigen, ie, ie, *intr.* rise upward, ascend

auf=tauchen, *intr.* rise up,
emerge from (*the water*)

auf=türmen, *tr.* pile up; aufge=
türmt towering

aufwärts upward

Auge, *n.* -s, -n eye

aus=blicken, *intr.* look out

aus=brennen, brannte, gebrannt,
intr. cease burning *or* glow-
ing, burn out

aus=graben, u, a; ä, *tr.* dig out

aus=klingen, a, u, *intr.* cease
sounding

aus=löschen, o, o; i, *intr.* be extinguished, go out

aus=machen, *tr.* settle

aus=reichen, *intr.* suffice, be
sufficient

aus=rufen, ie, u, *tr.* call out,
cry out

aus=ruhen, *intr.* rest; ausgeruht
haben be rested

aus=schauen, *intr.* look out

außen outside; von — from
without

aus=singen, a, u, *intr.* cease *or*
finish singing

aus=spannen, *tr.* stretch out,
spread

aus=steigen, ie, ie, *intr.* get out,
disembark

aus=strecken, *tr.* stretch out,
prostrate

aus=ziehen, zog, gezogen, *tr.*
undress; take off, pull off

B

Bach, *m.* ⸗e brook

baden, *tr. and intr.* (*refl.*) bathe

Bahn, *f.* -en path, track

bald soon; — ... — now
... now

Band, *m.* ⸗e volume

Band, *n.* ⸗er ribbon

Band, *n.* -e bond, fetter

bang fearful, afraid

bangen, *intr.* yearn

Bank, *f.* ⸗e bench

bannen, *tr.* charm, drive away

Banner, *n.* — banner

Barke, *f.* -n barque

Bart, *m.* ⸗e beard

Bau, *m.* -s, -ten structure,
building

Bauch, *m.* ⸗e belly, paunch

Bauer, *m.* -s *and* -n, -n farmer

Baum, *m.* ⸗e tree

bäumen, *refl.* rear, prance

beben, *intr.* tremble, shake

Becher, *m.* — cup, goblet

Beckenschlag, *m.* ⸗e clang of
cymbals

bedecken, *tr.* cover

bedeuten, *tr.* mean, portend

Bedeutung *f.* -en meaning

bedrohen, *tr.* threaten, menace

bedrücken, *tr.* oppress

beengen, *tr.* narrow in, oppress

beerdigen, *tr.* bury

Beet, *n.* -e bed (*in a garden*)

befragen, *tr.* question

befreien, *tr.* free, liberate

befreundet friendly

begegnen, *intr.* meet, pass

Begier, *f.* desire

beginnen, a, o, *tr.* begin

beglänzen, *tr.* illumine, cover with radiance

begleiten, *tr.* accompany

Begleiter, *m.* — one who accompanies a person, companion

beglücken, *tr.* make happy, bless with happiness

begraben, u, a; ä, *tr.* bury

begrenzen, *tr.* confine, limit

Behagen, *n.* content, delight

behalten, ie, a; ä, *tr.* retain, keep; das Wort — keep on speaking

Beharrung, *f.* perseverance, continuance

behend(e) nimble, agile

beherzt courageous, daring

beichten *tr.* confess

Bein, *n.* -e leg

beinah almost

beinern bony, skeleton

beisammen together

bekämpfen, *tr.* combat, resist

bekennen, bekannte, bekannt, *tr.* confess

beklommen oppressed

bellen, *intr.* bark

bemessen, ä, e; i, *tr.* measure

benebeln, *tr.* cover with fog; *p.p.* befuddled, drunk, made drowsy

bereit ready, prepared

bereiten, *tr.* prepare

Berg, *m.* -e mountain

bergen, a, o; i, *tr.* hide, shelter

Bergeshang, *m.* ⸚e mountain slope

Bergesrand, *m.* ⸚er edge *or* side of a mountain *or* hill

Bergesrücken, *m.* — mountain ridge *or* crest

berichten, *tr.* report

bersten, a (o), o; i, *intr.* burst, explode

beruhigen, *tr.* calm

berühren, *tr.* touch

besänftigen, *tr.* assuage

beschatten, *tr.* cast a shadow on, shade

beschauen, *tr.* view, look at

Bescheid, *m.* -e answer, response; — trinken pledge (*i.e., answer to a toast*)

bescheiden, ie, ie, *tr.* apportion, allot, destine; *refl.* moderate oneself, resign oneself to one's fate

Bescheiden, *n.* moderation, content, resignation

bescheinen, ie, ie, *tr.* illumine, shine upon

beschleichen, ĭ, ĭ, *tr.* steal upon

beschmutzen, *tr.* make dirty, sully

Beschützer, *m.* — protector

besiegen, *tr.* overcome, conquer

besingen, a, u, *tr.* sing about, praise in song

Besinnung, *f.* consciousness, reflection; — raubend robbing one of the power of reflection, sense destroying

besinnungslos unconscious

Besitz, *m.* possession

besitzen, besaß, besessen, *tr.* possess

bespiegeln, *refl.* gaze at oneself as in a mirror

besprechen, ä, o; i, *tr.* charm by magic words

besser better

bestehen, bestand, bestanden, (in), *intr.* consist (of)

beſtellen, *tr.* order, give a message

beſtrahlen, *tr.* shine upon, illumine

betäuben, *tr.* render unconscious; lame

beten, *intr.* pray

betören, *tr.* beguile, delude

betrügen, o, o, *tr.* deceive

Bett(e), *n.* -es, -en bed

Bettelkind, *n.* -er beggar child

betteln, *tr.* beg

Bettler, *m.* — beggar

beugen, *tr. and reflex.* bend, bow

bewachen, *tr.* guard, watch over

bewahren, *tr.* guard, keep

bewegen, *tr.* move, stir, agitate

beweinen, *tr.* lament, weep for

bewußt conscious of

bezeigen, *tr. and reflex.* show, manifest

bezwingen, a, u, *tr. and reflex.* conquer, suppress

biegen, o, o, *tr. and reflex.* bend

Biene, *f.* -n bee

Bier, *n.* -e beer

Bild, *n.* -er picture; image

bilden, *tr.* form

binden, a, u, *tr.* bind, tie

Birne, *f.* -n pear

bislang for the time being

bißchen bit, trifle

Bitte, *f.* -n request, prayer

blähen, *tr.* cause to bloat, distend

blank shining, bright

blasen, ie, a; ä, *tr. and intr.* blow

blaß pale

Blatt, *n.* -er leaf

blau blue, azure; im Blauen in the azure blue

Blau, *n.* azure of the sky

Bläue, *f.* blueness, azure

blauen, *intr.* appear blue, become blue

Blei, *n.* lead (*the metal*)

bleiben, ie, ie, *intr.* (ſ) remain

bleich pale

blenden, *tr.* blind, dazzle

Blick, *m.* -e glance, look

blicken, *intr.* look, gaze

blinken, *intr.* gleam, glisten

Blitz, *m.* -e lightning, flash of lightning

blitzen, *intr.* flash, gleam

Blitzesſchlag, *m.* -e stroke of lightning

blond blonde, fair

blühen, *intr.* blossom, bloom; blühend in the bloom of life

Bluht, *f. cf.* blühen bloom

Blume, *f.* -n flower

Blumengeſicht, *n.* -er blossom face

Blumengewind, *n.* -e wreath of flowers

Blut, *n.* blood

Blüte, *f.* -n blossom

bluten, *intr.* bleed

Blütendampf, *m.* -e haze of blossoms (Dampf steam, vapor)

blütenreich rich in blossoms, full of blossoms

Blütenſchimmer, *m.* — shimmer of blossoms

blutig bloody

Blutſtrahl, *m.* -s, -en stream of blood

Boden, *m.* soil, ground; space below the rafters

Bodenluke, *f.* -n trapdoor opening into the attic

Bogen, *m.* bow, arch

Bombardon, *n.* bombardon

Boot, *n.* -e *and* Böte boat

Born, *m.* –e fount, spring
böse evil, wicked
Bösewicht, *m.* –er rascal, wrong doer
brauchen, *tr.* use, need, be in need of (*with genitive*)
brauen, *tr. and intr.* brew, ferment
braun brown
brausen, *intr.* roar; rustle
Brautfest, *n.* –e bridal festival
brechen, ā, o; i, *tr.* break; pick (eine Blume); das Auge bricht the eye grows dim in death
brennen, brannte, gebrannt, *intr.* burn
Brot, *n.* –e bread
brotwarm warm as new-baked bread
Brücke, *f.* –n bridge
Bruder, *m.* ⸚ brother
Brudergruß, *m.* ⸚e brotherly greeting
Brunnen, *m.* — well, fountain, spring
brünstig ardent, eager
Brust, *f.* ⸚e breast
Brut, *f.* –en brood
Bube, *m.* –n knave, boy, fellow
Buch, *n.* ⸚er book
Buche, *f.* –n beech
buchendunkel dark with beeches
Buchengang, *m.* ⸚e path bordered by beeches
Bucht, *f.* –en bay
Buhle, *f.* –n sweetheart; *m.* lover
Buhler, *m.* — lover, wooer
Bühne, *f.* –n stage
bunt of various colors
Bursche, *m.* –en (–e) fellow, youth, boy

Busch, *m.* ⸚e shrub, bush
Busen, *m.* — bosom

C

Chor, *m.* ⸚e chorus, choir
christlich Christian
Christus, *m.* –i, –o, –um Christ

D

Dach, *n.* ⸚er roof
Dachgestühl(e), *n.* –e rafters
daheim at home
dahin thither
dahin=strecken, *tr.* stretch out
damit with it *or* them
dämmern, *intr.* spread a feeble light (*used of the coming of dawn or dusk*)
Dämmerschein, *m.* –e twilight
dämm(e)rig dusky
Dämmerung, *f.* twilight, dawn
dämpfen, *tr.* subdue
Dank, *m.* thanks, gratitude; zu — so as to merit thanks *or* meet approval
daran at it, beside it
darben, *intr.* suffer want
dar=bieten, o, o, *tr.* offer
dar=bringen, brachte, gebracht, *tr.* offer, present, sacrifice
darob on that account
darüber=gehen, ging, gegangen, *intr.* surpass; es geht mir nichts darüber I prize nothing more highly
da=sein, *intr.* be present
Dasein, *n.* existence
da=stehen, stand, gestanden, *intr.* be *or* stand there
dauern, *intr.* last, endure, continue
dazu besides

dazwischen in between

Decke, f. -n covering, blanket; ceiling, roof

decken, tr. cover

Degen, m. — sword

Degenknauf, m. ⁼e pommel of the sword's hilt

Deingedenken, n. thinking of you

Demut, f. humility

denken, dachte, gedacht, tr. think; jemandes or an jemanden — think of someone

dereinst some (future) day, in days to come

derweil the while that (archaic for während while)

deutlich clear

deutsch German

dicht dense, close

dichten, tr. compose or create in poetry; im Leben oder Dichten in life or verse

Dichter, m. — poet

dick thick, fat, plump

dienen, intr. (with dat.) serve

Dienst, m. -e service; ich bin zu — I am at your service

Dirne, f. -n lass, girl

Distel, f. -n thistle

Dolde, f. -n umbel, cluster of blossoms

Donner, m. — thunder

donnern, intr. thunder

Donnerkeule, f. -n thunder club

doppelt double, twofold

Dorf, n. ⁼er village

dort there, yonder

Drache, m. -n dragon

drall buxom

drängen, tr. press

draus = daraus out of, therefrom

draußen outside, without

drehen, tr. turn

drein= (or darein=) blicken | intr. gaze, look on
drein=schauen |

dreist bold

dringen, a, u, intr. press, penetrate; in jemanden — importune

drinnen within

droben up there

drohen, tr. and intr. threaten

dröhnen, intr. reverberate

Drossel, f. -n thrush

drüben yonder

drücken tr. press

drunten down below, down there

Duft, m. ⁼e odor, fragrance; haze

duften intr. be fragrant, spread fragrance

duftig fragrant; hazy, airy

dulden, tr. bear, tolerate

dumpf dull, hollow (of sound)

dumpfbrausend with a hollow roar

dunkel dark

dunkeln, intr. grow dark

dünn thin

durchbeben, tr. throb through

durchdringen, a, u, tr. penetrate

durcheilen, tr. hasten or pass through quickly

durchstreichen, i, i, tr. ramble, roam through

durchwandeln, tr. wander through

dürftig scanty, sparse

dürr withered, dry

Durst, m. thirst

Dursteswut, f. rage of thirst

durstüberquält overtortured by thirst

düſter dark, gloomy
Düſter, *n.* gloom, darkness
düſterrot gloomy red

E

eben *for* ſoeben just
echt genuine, real
Ecke, *f.* -n corner
edel noble
Efeu, *m.*, *n.* ivy
ehe before
Ehre, *f.* -n honor
Ehrenkreuz, *n.* -e cross of honor
Eiche, *f.* -n oak
eigen peculiar
Eigentum, *n.* ⸗er possession
eilig hasty, hurried
ein⸗fallen, ie, a; ä, *intr.* interrupt
ein⸗kehren, *intr.* enter, turn in
ein⸗läuten, *tr.* ring in
ein⸗legen, *tr.* lay *or* put in; ein⸗
  gelegte Ruder oars dipped
  into the water
einmal once (upon a time)
einſam lonely, alone
ein⸗ſcharren, *tr.* bury hurriedly
  (ſcharren = scrape, scratch)
ein⸗ſchenken, *tr.* pour in *or* out;
  Wein — fill the glasses with
  wine
ein⸗ſchlafen, ie, a; ä, *intr.* fall
  asleep
ein⸗ſchlummern, *intr.* fall asleep;
  wieder — return to slumber
Einſiedel, *m.* — hermit
einſt sometime, once upon a
  time
ein⸗ſteigen, ie, ie, *intr.* get in
einſtmals once upon a time
eintönig monotonous
ein⸗treten, a, e; tritt, *intr.* enter,
  step in; occur

einzeln single
einzig single, unique, only
Eis, *n.* ice
Eiſen, *n.* — iron
elend wretched
Elfe, *f.* -n elf
empfangen, i, a; ä, *tr.* receive
empfinden, a, u, *tr.* feel
empor upward
Ende *n.* -s, -n end; an allen
  -n everywhere; am — finally
enden, *intr.* end, stop
endlos endless, unending
Engelland = England, *n.* England
engliſch English
entbrennen, entbrannte (ent⸗
  brannte), entbrannt, *intr.* start
  to burn *or* to glow
entdecken, *tr.* discover
entfachen, *tr.* enkindle
entfahren, u, a; ä, *intr.* escape,
  slip from
entfärben, *tr.* decolorate; *refl.*
  lose color, fade
entfernen, *tr.* remove; *refl.*
  withdraw
entfliehen, o, o, *intr.* escape
entgegen⸗ragen, *intr.* project *or*
  loom up against
entgelten, a, o; i, *tr.* suffer *or*
  atone for
entkleiden, *tr. and refl.* undress
entlang (*prep. with acc.*) along
entlegen distant, far off
Entſagung, *f.* -en renunciation
entſchlafen, ie, a; ä, *intr.* go to
  sleep
entſchleiern, *tr.* unveil
entſchweben, *intr.* soar away
Entſetzen, *n.* terror
entſpringen, a, u, *intr.* escape
entſtellen, *tr.* disfigure

entzwei=fpringen, a, u, *intr.* burst asunder

Erbe, *m.* –n heir

erblaffen, *intr.* turn pale; die

erbleichen, ĭ, ĭ, *intr.* turn pale

erbliden, *tr.* catch sight of

erblinden, *intr.* grow blind

erbbefchmutzt "earth sullied," covered with earth

Erde, *f.* –n earth

erdenken, erbachte, erbacht, *tr.* devise, invent

Erdenziehen, *n.* earthly journeying

erfahren, u, a; ä, *tr.* experience, learn

erfinden, a, u, *tr.* invent (*archaic for* finden find)

erfreulich joyful, pleasing; — fein be a thing of joy

ergießen, ŏ, ŏ, *tr.* pour forth, shed

erglänzen, *intr.* shine forth

ergötzlich amusing

ergreifen, iff, iff, *tr.* seize, grasp

erhalten, ie, a; ä, *tr.* preserve, keep; receive

erheben, o, o, *tr.* raise, uplift; *refl.* rise

Erinnerung, *f.* –en memory, remembrance

erfalten, *intr.* grow cool

erkennen, erfannte, erfannt, *tr.* recognize

erflingen, a, u, *intr.* resound

erlernen, *tr.* learn

erlefen, a, e; ie, *tr.* choose

erleuchten, *tr.* illumine

erliegen, a, e, *intr.* succumb, be defeated

erlöfchen, o, o; i, *intr.* go out, be extinguished

ermatten, *intr.* grow weary

ermüden, *intr.* grow tired

erneuen, *tr. and refl.* renew

ernft earnest, serious

Ernft, *m.* earnestness, seriousness

Ernte, *f.* –n harvest

erquiden, *tr.* refresh

Erquidung, *f.* –en refreshment

erreichen, *tr.* reach, attain

erfchallen, *weak or* o, o, *intr.* resound, ring out

erfcheinen, ie, ie, *intr.* appear

erfchlagen, u, a; ä, *tr.* slay, kill

erfchreden, ā, o; i, *intr.* be terrified *or* frightened

erfchwingen, a, u, *refl.* take wing *or* flight

erftarren, *intr.* grow numb, be paralyzed, turn rigid

erftechen, ā, o; i, *tr.* kill by stabbing, stab *or* run through with a knife *or* sword

erfteigen, ie, ie, *tr.* climb

erfticken, *tr. and intr.* smother, choke, suffocate

erwachen, *intr.* awaken

erwählen, *tr.* choose

erwarten, *tr.* await, wait for

erweifen, ie, ie, *tr.* prove; render, bestow upon

erweiten, *tr. and refl.* widen, expand, grow

Erz, *n.* –e ore, metal, bronze

erzählen, *tr.* tell, relate

effen, aß, gegeffen; ißt, *tr.* eat

etwa perhaps; perchance

Eule, *f.* –n owl

ewig eternal

Ewigfeit, *f.* –en eternity

F

fachen, *tr.* fan, kindle

Fadel, *f.* –n torch

Fahne, *f.* -n flag

fahren, u, a; ä, *intr.* move, journey, go

fallen, ie, a; ä, *intr.* fall, drop; etwas fällt jemandem in die Augen something strikes one's gaze

falten, *tr.* fold

Falter, *m.* — butterfly

fangen, i, a; ä, *tr.* catch, capture

Farbe, *f.* -n color

fassen, *tr.* grasp, take hold of, seize, understand

Fassung, *f.* capacity

fast almost

Faust, *f.* ⸚e fist

Fehl, *m.* -e wrong, guilt, blemish

fehlen, *intr.* lack; mir fehlt etwas I lack something

Feier, *f.* -n festal celebration

feierlich festal, solemn

feiern, *intr.* rest (*from one's labor*)

feig cowardly

fein fine, delicate, fair

Feind, *m.* -e enemy

Feld, *n.* -er field

Fels, *m.* -ens, -en rock, cliff

Felsenbank, *f.* ⸚e bench of rock

Felsenriff, *n.* -e reef

Felsenschlucht, *f.* -en rocky ravine

felsig rocky

Felswand, *f.* ⸚e wall of rock, precipice

Fenster, *n.* — window

Ferge, *m.* -n ferryman

fern far, distant; (*with dat.*) far from

Ferne, *f.* -n distance

fernher from afar

fernhin far off

Fest, *n.* -e festival, celebration

fest(e) firm, fast, strong

fest=halten, ie, a; ä, *tr.* hold (firmly)

feucht moist, wet

Feuer, *n.* — fire

Feuerleiter, *f.* -n fire ladder

feurig fiery, ardent

Fichte, *f.* -n pine

Fieber, *n.* — fever

fieberwild wild *or* raging with fever

finden, a, u, *tr.* find

Finger, *m.* — finger

Fink, *m.* -en finch

finster dark, gloomy

Finsternis, *f.* -isse darkness

Firn, *m.* -e last year's snow; mountains topped with perpetual snow

Firneschein, *m.* glow of the snow-capped mountains

Fisch, *m.* -e fish

fischen, *tr.* fish

Fischer, *m.* — fisherman

flach flat, level

Fläche, *f.* -n surface

flämisch Flemish

Flamme, *f.* -n flame

flattern, *intr.* flutter

flechten, o, o; i, *tr.* braid, plait, intertwine

flehen, *intr.* beseech, implore, pray (um etwas for something)

fleißig industrious, busy

fliegen, o, o, *intr.* fly

fliehen, o, o, *intr.* flee; *tr.* flee from

fließen, ŏ, ŏ, *intr.* flow

flimmern, *intr.* glitter, glimmer

flink quick, swift, nimble

Flinte, *f.* -n gun, rifle

flirren, *intr.* vibrate

Flitter, *m.* — spangle, tinsel; empty pomp; adornment

Flor, *m.* veil; bloom

Flötist, *m.* -en flute player

Fluch, *m.* ⸗e curse

flüchtig fleeting, fleeing

Flug, *m.* ⸗e flight

Flügel, *m.* — wing, pinion

Flügelschlag, *m.* ⸗e flap *or* beat of wings

Flügelwehn, *n.* wafting of wings

Flur, *f.* -en field, plain

Fluß, *m.* ⸗e river

flußüberwärts across the river

flüstern, *intr.* whisper

Flüsterwort, *n.* -e whispered word

Flut, *f.* -en flood

fluten, *intr.* stream, surge

Flutengrab, *n.* ⸗er grave beneath the water

fodern = fordern, *tr.* demand

Föhn, *m.* -e south wind

folgen, *intr.* (*with dat.*) follow

fördern, *tr.* advance, hasten

Form, *f.* -en form

formen, *tr.* form

Forschbegierde, *f.* desire to learn *or* investigate

forschen, *intr.* inquire into, search

fort, *adv.* away; *sep. pref.* (1) *with verbs expressing a change of place* away, e.g., fort⸗ ziehen journey away, depart; forttragen carry away; (2) on, to continue to, *e.g.*, fortsingen keep on singing, continue to sing

fort und fort on and on

fragen, *tr.* ask

Frager, *m.* — questioner

frank frank

Frankreich, *n.* France

Frau, *f.* -en woman, wife, Mrs.

Fräulein, *n.* — Miss, unmarried young lady, (*archaic*) young lady of rank

frech insolent, audacious

frei free

frei⸗geben, a, e; i, *tr.* set free, release

Freiheit, *f.* -en freedom, liberty

fremd foreign, alien, strange

Fremdling, *m.* -e stranger

Freude, *f.* -n joy

Freudenrechnung, *f.* -en account of joys

freudig joyful

freuen, *refl.* rejoice, be happy; *tr.* make rejoice, make happy

Freund, *m.* -e friend

freundlich friendly, kindly

Frevel, *m.* — outrage, wrong

freventlich outrageous, nefarious

Friede, *m.* -ens peace

Friedenswunder, *n.* — miracle of peace, peaceful miracle

friedfertig, friedlich peaceful

frisch fresh

froh merry; (*with gen.*) happy in

fröhlich joyful, glad

fromm pious, reverent, God-fearing

frommen, *intr.* (*with dat.*) be useful, avail *or* profit

Frucht, *f.* ⸗e grain, fruit

früh early

Frühe, *f.* dawn, early morning

Frühling, *m.* -e spring

Frühstück, *n.* -e breakfast

fügen, *tr.* arrange, ordain

fühlen, *tr. and intr.* (*refl.*) feel

führen, *tr.* lead; einen Schlag — deal a blow

Führer, *m.* — leader, guide
füllen, *tr.* fill
funkeln, *intr.* sparkle
Funken, *m.* — spark
furchtbar terrible
fürder onward
fürsichtig = vorsichtig prudent, cautious
Fürstin, *f.* –nen princess
Fuß, *m.* ⸚e foot
Fußgestell, *n.* –e pedestal

G

Gabe, *f.* –n gift
Gang, *m.* ⸚e course; walk, stride
ganz whole, entire
gänzlich entire
gar very, utterly
Garbe, *f.* –n sheaf
Garten, *m.* ⸚ garden
Gasse, *f.* –n narrow street
Gast, *m.* ⸚e guest
Gastfreund, *m.* –e *person connected with another by ties of hospitable friendship*
gastlich hospitable
Gaul, *m.* ⸚e horse of inferior breed, nag
Gazelle, *f.* –n gazelle
Gebein, *n.* (*collective*) — bones, frame
Gebell, *n.* barking
geben, a, e; i, *tr.* give
Gebet, *n.* –e prayer
Gebrüll, *n.* roar, roaring
Gedanke, *m.* –n thought
gedankenvoll full of thought, absorbed in thought
gedeihen, ie, ie, *intr.* thrive
gedrang narrow (*from* drängen)
Gedränge, *n.* — throng, surging crowd

Gedröhne, *n.* — resounding *or* sonorous pealing
geduldig patient
gefährden, *tr.* endanger
gefallen, ie, a; ä, *intr.* please; es gefällt mir I like it
Gefieder, *n.* — plumage
Gefild(e), *n.* –e field
Geflügel, *n.* birds, winged creatures
geflügelt winged
gefrieren, o, o, *intr.* freeze, congeal
Gefühl, *n.* –e feeling, emotion
Gefunkel, *n.* sparkling, glittering
Gegend, *f.* –en region, country
gegenwärtig present
geheim secret
Geheimnis, *n.* –isse secret
gehen, ging, gegangen, *intr.* go
geheuer (*only with negative* nicht) uncanny
Geier, *m.* — vulture
Geierflug, *m.* ⸚e flight of vultures
Geißel, *f.* –n scourge, lash
Geist, *m.* –er spirit, ghost, phantom
geistern, *intr.* spook
Gelände, *n.* — open fields
gelassen calm, gentle
Geläut(e), *n.* –e set of bells, chime; ringing, pealing (*of bells*)
Geliebter, *m.* Geliebte, *f.* beloved, lover, sweetheart
gelinde gentle, mild, soft
gellen, *intr.* sound shrill
geloben, *tr.* promise, vow
gelten, a, o; i, *intr.* be valid, be worth; concern; es gilt mir it is for me; es gilt uns heut

zu rühren our duty today
is, *etc.*

Gemach, *n.* ⸚er room, chamber

gemachsam, *adv.* leisurely

Gemahl, *n.* spouse, consort

Gemüt, *n.* -er feeling, soul,
heart

genau exact

genießen, o, o, *tr.* enjoy

Genoß *or* Genosse, *m.* -n companion

Genüge, *f.* sufficiency, content

genügen, *intr.* suffice

genüg(e)sam content; contentedly

Geräusch *n.* -e noise

gerecht just

Gericht, *n.* -e judgment; tribunal

Gerippe, *n.* — skeleton

gerne, *adv.* gladly; (*with verb*)
like to

Gesang, *m.* ⸚e song

geschehen, a, e; ie, (ſ) *intr.* happen

Geschichte, *f.* -n story

Geschlecht, *n.* -er generation;
race

Geschmeide, *n.* — jewelry

geschmeidig supple, agile

Geschrei, *n.* cry, shout

Geschwader, *n.* — squadron

geschwind quick, swift

Geschwister, *n. pl.* brother(s)
and sister(s); *n. sing.* (*rare*)
sister

Geselle, *m.* -n journeyman, fellow, youth

gesellen, *tr. and refl.* join, ally;
dicht gesellt closely together

Gesetz, *n.* -e law

Gesicht, *n.* -er face

Gesinde, *n.* servants

Gespenst, *n.* -er phantom, ghost

Gestalt, *f.* -en form, figure

gestehen, gestand, gestanden, *tr.*
confess

Gestein, *n.* -e large rocks *or*
stones; stony debris *or* ruins;
jewels

Gestirn, *n.* -e star

Gesträuch, *n.* -e shrubs, bushes

gesund healthy

Gesundheit, *f.* -en health

Getrabe, *n.* trotting

getreu faithful

getrost confident

Gewächs, *n.* -e plant

gewaffnet armed

gewähren, *tr.* grant

Gewalt, *f.* -en force, violence

gewaltig powerful, mighty

Gewand, *n.* ⸚er garment, robe

Gewerbe, *n.* — profession,
trade

gewichtig weighty, momentous

Gewimmel, *n.* crowd, crush,
throng

gewinnen, a, o, *tr.* win, gain

Gewissen, *n.* — conscience

Gewitter, *n.* — thunderstorm

gewogen kindly disposed to

gewohnt accustomed

Gewölbe, *n.* — vault

Gewühle, *n.* tumult, throng

Gezelt, *n.* -e (*poet. for* Zelt) tent

gießen, o, o, *tr.* pour

giftgeschwollen swollen by poison, venom filled

Gipfel, *m.* — top (*mountain
top*)

Gitter, *n.* — lattice, grating,
screen

Glanz, *m.* splendor

glänzen, *intr.* shine, gleam

Glas, *n.* ⸚er glass

glatt smooth

Glaube, *m.* -ns, -n faith, belief

glauben, *tr. and intr.* believe

gleich like (*with dat.*); ein gleiches another

gleich *for* sogleich at once

gleichen, i, i, *intr.* (*with dat.*) be similar *or* like

gleichgeschwungen having an equal swing

Gleis, *n.* -e (*for* Geleise) track

gleiten, itt, itt, *intr.* glide

Glied, *n.* -er limb; ins — treten fall into line

glimmen, o, o, *intr.* glimmer, glow

Glocke, *f.* -n bell

Glück, *n.* fortune, happiness

glücklich fortunate, happy

glühen, *intr.* glow

Glut, *f.* -en glow, fire

Gnade, *f.* -n mercy, grace

gnaden, *intr.* (*with dat.*) be merciful to

Gold, *n.* gold

golden gold, golden

Goldorange, *f.* -n golden orange

gönnen, *tr.* not begrudge, be willing to let have

Gosse, *f.* -n gutter

gotisch Gothic

Gott, *m.* ̈er God

Götterfreund, *m.* -e friend of the gods (*i.e.*, beloved by the gods)

Gottheit, *f.* -en divinity, God

Grab, *n.* ̈er grave; zu Grabe bringen bury

graben, u, a; ä, *tr.* dig

Graben, *m.* ̈ ditch, moat

Gräbergraber, *m.* — grave digger

Grabesruh(e), *f.* peace of the grave

Grad, *m.* -e degree

Gram, *m.* woe, grief

Gras, *n.* ̈er grass

grasen, *intr.* graze

grau gray

grauen, *intr. and refl.* be afraid; mich (oder mir) graut I shudder, feel horror *or* awe

grauen turn gray; es graut it dawns

Grauen, *n.* horror, awe; süßes Graun thrills of mysterious sweet awe

grauenvoll full of horror, appalling

graulicht grayish

graus horrible, dreadful

Graus, *m.* horror

grausen, *intr.* have a feeling of horror; mir graus(e)t I shudder

Greis, *m.* -e aged man

Grenadier, *m.* -e grenadier

Grenze, *f.* -n limit, border

Grieche, *m.* -n Greek

Griechenland, *n.* Greece

Grille, *f.* -n cricket

grinsen, *intr.* grin

Groom, *m.* groom (*English*)

groß large, big, great

Gruft, *f.* ̈e tomb, grave, cavern

grün green

Grund, *m.* ̈e bottom, earth, ground

grünen, *intr.* grow, flourish

Gruß, *m.* ̈e greeting

grüßen, *tr.* greet; seid mir gegrüßt I greet you; — lassen send greetings

gülden golden

Gunst, *f.* favor, good will, kindness

günstig favorable

Guß, m. Güsse pouring (of molten metal)

gut good; es gut haben fare well

Güte, f. goodness

H

Haar, n. -e hair

Habe, f. possessions, belongings; mein Hab' und Gut all I have and own

Habsucht, f. avarice

Hafen, m. ⸚ harbor, port

haften, intr. cling

Hag, m. -e hedge; wood, grove

Hahn, m. ⸚e cock, rooster

Hain, m. -e (poet.) grove

halb half

Halle, f. -n hall

hallen, intr. resound

Halm, m. -e stalk of grain or grass

Hals, m. ⸚e throat

halten, ie, a; ä, tr. hold, contain; celebrate; intr. stop, halt

halt-machen, intr. stop

Hand, f. ⸚e hand

hangen, i, a; ä, intr. hang, cling

Harfe, f. -n harp

Harfenspieler m. — harp player, minstrel

Harmonie, f. -en harmony

harren, intr. wait, tarry

hart hard

haschen, tr. and intr. clutch; reach for quickly

hassen, tr. hate

Hast, f. haste, hurry

Hauch, m. -e breath

hauchen, intr. breathe

hauen, hieb, gehauen, tr. hew, strike

Haupt, n. ⸚er head

Hauptmann, m., pl. —leute captain

Haus, n. ⸚er house

heben, o (u), o, tr. raise; sich klarer — stand out more sharply

Heer, n. -e army

heften, tr. fasten, attach

heftig violent

hegen, tr. cherish, protect

hehr high, noble, lofty

hei hurrah! hey!

Heide, f. -n heath; heather

Heiland, m. Saviour

heilig holy, sacred

Heiligkeit, f. sacredness, holiness

Heimat, f. -en home

Heimatflur, f. -en home, native fields

heimatlich homelike

heim-bringen, brachte, gebracht, tr. bring home

Heimchen, n. — cricket

heim-gehen, ging, gegangen, intr. go home; die

heim-kehren, intr. return home

heimlich secret

Heimlichkeit, f. -en secrecy

heiraten, tr. marry

heiß hot

heißen, ie, ei, tr. name, call; intr. be called; ich heiße my name is

Heiterkeit, f. -en cheer, cheerfulness

Held, m. -en hero

helfen, a, o; i, intr. help

Helikon, n. helicon

hell bright, clear

her hither

herab down, down from

heran hither, up to

heran-kommen, ā, o, *intr.* approach

herauf up here, upward

herauf-klimmen, o, o; *intr.* climb upward

herb harsh, bitter, acrid

herbei hither

Herbſt, *m.* -e autumn, fall

Herd, *m.* -e hearth

Herde, *f.* -n herd

Herdgetön, *n.* chime of herds

herein in here, into, in

herfür = **hervor**

hernieder down

hernieder-lachen, *intr.* laugh down from on high

Herr, *m.* -en master; gentleman; (*in address* Sir; *with name* Mr.); the Lord

herrlich glorious, splendid

herunter down, downward

herunter-ſteigen, ie, ie, *intr.* descend

hervor forth, forth from

hervor-rauſchen, *intr.* come forth, *or* emerge from with a rustling sound

Herz, *n., gen.* -ens, *dat.* -en, *pl.* -en heart

herzlieb very dear *or* lovable

Herzliebchen, *n.* sweetheart

Herzog, *m.* ⸗e duke

Heu, *n.* hay

heulen, *intr.* howl

heute today

heutig, *adj. from* **heute; am heutigen Tag** on this day

Himmel, *m.* — sky, the heavens; Heaven

himmelan heavenward

himmliſch heavenly

hin along, thither, toward

hinab down, downward

hinauf up, upward

hinaus out, hence; — **über** *with acc.* beyond

hinein into, in; — **in** (*with acc.*) *or* **zu** — into

Hintergrund, *m.* ⸗e background

hinüber over, across

hinunter down

hinunter-ſpülen, *tr.* wash *or* rinse down

hinzu-ſetzen, *tr.* add

Hirſch, *m.* -e deer

Hirt, *m.* -en herdsman, shepherd

hoch high

hochgetürmt high-towering

hochüber across on high

Hochzeit, *f.* -en wedding

Hof, *m.* ⸗e yard, court; home

hoffen, *tr. and intr.* hope; (**auf** for)

Hoffnung, *f.* -en hope

Höfling, *m.* -e courtier

Höhe, *f.* -n height

höhen, *tr.* heighten

hohl hollow

Höhle, *f.* -n cave, cavern

hold gracious, fair, sweet

holländiſch Dutch

Hölle, *f.* -n hell

Höllenſchein, *m.* infernal light *or* glow

Hollunder, *m.* — (*for* **Holunder**) lilac, elder

horchen, *intr.* listen, hearken

hören, *tr.* hear

Hörer, *m.* — listener

Horn, *n.* ⸗er horn

hüben on this side

hübſch pretty

Huf, *m.* -e hoof

Hügel, *m.* — hill

huldigen, *intr.* do homage to

Hülle, f. -n wrap, covering
Hund, m. -e dog
hungrig hungry
hüpfen, intr. hop, jump
husch! hush! 'sh!
Hut, m. ⸚e hat
Hütte, f. -n hut, cottage
Hymnus, m. chant, solemn song

J

immer always
immerdar always, forever
immerhin at all events
inmitten in the midst of
innerlich inward, within
innig fervent, heartfelt
Insel, f. -n island
irdisch earthly, of this world
irgend ein any
irr confused; erring
irren, intr. and refl. err, go astray

J

jagen, tr. hunt
Jäger, m. — hunter
Jahr, n. -e year
jahrlang through the years
Jammer, m. lament, distress
jammern, intr. lament, moan, wail
jauchzen, intr. cry out with joy, exult
je ever
jetzt now
jetzo } old forms for jetzt
jetzund }
Joch, n. -e yoke
Johanneswürmchen, n. — glow-worm
jubeln, intr. rejoice, jubilate

Jugend, f. youth
jung young
Junge, m. (adj. used as a noun) boy, swain
Jungfrau, f. -en maiden
Jüngling, m. -e young man, youth
Juni, m. June
Junker, m. — squire
just by chance

K

kahl bare, bald
Kahn, m. ⸚e boat
Kaiser, m. — emperor
Kamerad, m. -en comrade
Kamm, m. ⸚e comb
kämmen, tr. comb
Kammer, f. -n chamber, room
Kampf, m. ⸚e battle, contest
Kanone, f. -n cannon
Kapelle, f. -n chapel
Kapuze, f. -n cap, hood, cowl
karg sparse, meager
Kasten, m. ⸚ box
kaum hardly, barely
keck bold
Kehle, f. -n throat
kehren, tr. and intr. (refl.) turn, return
Kelch, m. -e calyx, cup
kennen, kannte, gekannt, tr. know
Kerze, f. -n candle
kerzenhell made bright by candles
Kette, f. -n chain
keuchen, intr. gasp, breathe with difficulty
kichern, intr. laugh softly, chuckle
Kind, n. -er child (In many compounds Kinder- is best

rendered by childhood, *e.g.*,
Kinderfrieden peace of childhood)

kindlich childlike

Kinn, *n.* -e chin

Kirche, *f.* -n church

Kirchhof, *m.* ⁼e churchyard

Kissen, *n.* — pillow

Kiste, *f.* -n chest

Klage, *f.* -n complaint, plaint;
accusation

klagen, *intr.* complain, make
lament

kläglich pitiable

Klang, *m.* ⁼e sound

klappen, *intr.* clap, click

klar clear, bright

Kleid, *n.* -er dress, garment

kleiden, *tr.* dress, clothe

klein small, little

Kleinigkeit, *f.* -en trifle

klettern, *intr.* climb

klingen, α, u, *intr.* resound,
sound

klirren, *intr.* clatter, clank;
rattle

klopfen, *intr.* rap, knock

Kluft, *f.* ⁼e cleft, chasm

klug clever, intelligent, wise

Knabe, *m.* -n boy

knallen, *intr.* crack

Knäuel, *m.* — ball of thread;
entanglement

Knecht, *m.* -e servant

Knie, *n.* -e knee

knieen, *intr.* kneel

knistern, *intr.* crackle

Knochen, *m.* — bone

Knospe, *f.* -n bud

kommen, ā, o, *intr.* come

König, *m.* -e king (*In compounds* Königs⁼ *is often best
rendered by* royal, *e.g.*, Königs⁼

mahl, *n.* royal feast *or*
banquet)

Kopf, *m.* ⁼e head

Korn, *n.* grain, "corn" (*the
chief grain of a country; in
Germany rye or wheat; with
the pl.* Körner = *single seed
of grain*)

kosen, *intr. and tr.* fondle, caress

Kraft, *f.* ⁼e strength, power

kräftig strong

Krähe, *f.* -n crow

krähen, *intr.* crow; scream, cry
out

Kranich, *m.* -e crane

Kranichzug, *m.* ⁼e flight *or* flock
of cranes on wing

krank ill, sick

kränken, *tr.* grieve, wound

Kranz, *m.* ⁼e wreath, garland

Kraut, *n.* ⁼er plant; *collective*
plants, herbage

Kreis, *m.* -e circle

kreischen, *intr.* screech

Kreuz, *n.* -e cross, crucifix

Kreuzbild, *n.* -er image of the
crucified Saviour

Krieg, *m.* -e war

Krieger, *m.* — warrior

Krone, *f.* -n crown

Krug, *m.* ⁼e pitcher, jug

Krümlein (*dim. of* Krume, *f.*) —
crumb

Kuchen, *m.* — cake

Kugel, *f.* -n bullet, ball

kühl cool

kühlen, *tr.* cool

kühn bold

Kummer, *m.* worry, care

kummervoll filled with care

Kunde, *f.* lore, news

kund⁼machen, *tr.* make known,
announce

künftig future
Kunst, f. ̈-e art
Kunstgebild, n. -e work of art
Künstler m. — (Künstlerin, f.)
    artist
Kuppel, f. -n cupola, dome
kurz short, brief
Kuß, m. ̈-e kiss
küssen, tr. kiss
Küste, f. -en coast

L

laben, tr. refresh
Lache, f. -n pool, puddle
lächeln, intr. smile
lachen, intr. laugh
laden, u, a; lädt, tr. load
Lager, n. — couch
Laken, n. — sheet
Lampe, f. -n lamp
Land, n. ̈-er (poet. pl. Lande)
    land, country
Landesenge, f. -n isthmus
Landschaft, f. -en landscape
lang long
langsam slow
längst long since
Lanze, f. -n lance
Lärm, m. noise
Last, f. -en burden
Laterne, f. -n lantern
lau lukewarm, mild
Laub, n. foliage
Laube, f. -n arbor
lauern, intr. (auf with acc.) wait
    eagerly or greedily for some-
    thing; lie in wait for, lurk
    for
Lauf, m. course
laufen, ie, au; äu, intr. run
Laune, f. -n whim, humor
lauschen, intr. listen

laut loud
Laut, m. -e sound
Laute, f. -n lute
lauter pure, nothing but
lautlos soundless
leben, intr. live; lebe wohl fare-
    well
Leben, n. — life
lebendig alive, living
lebenlos lifeless
Lebewohl, n. farewell
leer empty, vacant; meaning-
    less, idle
leeren, tr. empty
legen, tr. lay, place, put; refl.
    lie down
lehnen, tr. and refl. lean
Leib, m. -er body
Leiblied, n. -er favorite song
Leiche, f. -n corpse
Leichenchor, m. ̈-e funeral choir
leichenfarb livid (color of a
    corpse)
Leichenzug, m. ̈-e funeral pro-
    cession
Leichnam, m. -e corpse
leicht light (not heavy)
leichtgläubig credulous
Leid, n. -es, -en grief, sorrow;
    wrong, injury; pain
leiden, itt, itt, tr. suffer, endure
Leier, f. -n lyre
leise soft (not loud)
Lende, f. -n loin
Lenz, m. -e spring
Lerche, f. -n lark
Lerchenwirbel, m. — thrill
    (song) of larks
Lerchenzug, m. ̈-e flight or flock
    of larks
lernen, tr. learn
Lese, f. -n gleaning, harvest
lesen, a, e; ie, tr. read

leuchten, *intr.* shine, glow, gleam

Leute, *pl.* people

Leutnant, *m.* –s lieutenant

licht light, bright

Licht, *n.* -er light; candle

Lid, *n.* -er eyelid

lieb dear, sweet, beloved; (*superlative used as a noun*) der (die) Liebste dearest, beloved

Liebchen, *n.* — sweetheart

Liebe, *f.* love

lieben, *tr.* love

Liebesschein, *m.* glow of love

liebevoll affectionate, full of love

lieb-haben, *tr.* hold dear, love

lieblich pretty, lovely, sweet

Liebling, *m.* -e pet, favorite, darling

liebselig blessed with love

Lied, *n.* -er song

Liedeslust, *f.* joy of song

liegen, a, e, *intr.* lie

Lilie, *f.* -n lily

lind gentle, mild

Linde, *f.* -n linden tree, basswood

links left; die Linke left hand

Lippe, *f.* -n lip

lispeln, *intr. and tr.* lisp

List, *f.* -en craft, cunning

Lob, *n.* praise

loben, *tr.* praise

Lobgesang, *m.* ⁼e song of praise

Locke, *f.* -n lock *or* tress of hair

locken, *tr.* entice, lure

Lorbeer, *m.* -s, -en laurel

Los, *n.* -e lot, fate

lose (los) loose; los werden get rid of

Lösegeld, *n.* -er ransom

lösen, *tr.* loosen, set free, release

Lotosblume, *f.* -n lotus flower

Luft, *f.* ⁼e air, breeze (*dim. always* = breeze)

luftig airy

Lust, *f.* ⁼e joy, desire; (*pl. usually* = lusts)

Lustgemach, *n.* ⁼er pleasure hall, festal hall

M

machen, *tr.* make

Macht, *f.* ⁼e power

Mädchen, *n.* — girl

Madonna, *f.* -en Madonna, the Holy Virgin

Magd, *f.* ⁼e maid, maiden

Mägdlein, *n.* — maiden, lassie

Mahd, *f.* -en mowing, hay crop

Mahl, *n.* -e *and* ⁼er repast, banquet, feast

Mähne, *f.* -n mane

Mähre, *f.* -n mare

Mai, *m.* May (*month*) (*In compounds often* Maien, *e.g.,* Maienglück, *n.* Maytime bliss)

Maid, *f.* (*poet.*) maiden

majestätisch majestic

Mal, *n.* -e time; zweimal two times

malen, *tr.* paint

Mandelbaum, *m.* ⁼e almond tree

Manen, *pl.* Manes, *i.e.*, spirits of the departed

Mann, *m.* ⁼er man

Männerwürde, *f.* -n manly dignity

Mantel, *m.* ⁼ mantle

Märchen, *n.* — fairy tale

märchenstill faëry still

Märe, *f.* -n tale

Marie, *f.* Mary
Mark, *n.* marrow
markig containing marrow;
(*fig.*) pithy, virile
Marmor, *m.* marble
Marmorbild, *n.* -er marble
image, statue
Marsch, *m.* ⸗e march
Matte, *f.* -n meadow (*especially*) mountain meadow
Mauer, *f.* -n wall
Maultier, *n.* -e mule
Meer, *n.* -e sea
meiden, ie, ie, *tr.* shun, avoid
meinen, *tr.* think, mean, be of
the opinion
Meister, *m.* — master
melden, *tr.* announce, make
known; mention
Melodei, *f.* (*poet. license for*
Melodie, *f.* -en) melody
melodisch melodious
Menge, *f.* -n crowd, throng
mengen, *tr. and refl.* mix, inter-
mingle
Mensch, *m.* -en human being,
man (*i.e.*, *homo*) (*In compounds* Menschen⸗ *often* =
human)
messen, ā, e; i, *tr.* measure, compare; sich mit jemandem —
try one's strength against
another's
Metall, *n.* -e metal
Miene, *f.* -n expression, mien,
air
mild mild, gentle
minder less
mischen, *tr.* mix, mingle
mit, *sep. pref.* along (*with
others*); *e.g.*, mit⸗gehen go along
Mitte, *f.* -n middle, midst
Mitternacht, *f.* ⸗e midnight

Moder, *m.* mould, decay
Mohn, *m.* poppy
Mond, *m.* -e moon
Mondnacht, *f.* ⸗e moonlit night
moosig mossy
Mord, *m.* -e murder
Mörder, *m.* — murderer
morgen tomorrow
Morgen, *m.* — morning
Morgenland, *n.* Orient
Morgenrot, *n.* Morgenröte, *f.* -n
the red morning sky, Aurora
Möwe, *f.* -n sea gull
müde tired; eine Sache — sein
be tired of a thing
Mühe, *f.* -n difficulty; en-
deavor
mühen, *tr.* weary
Mühle, *f.* -n mill
Mühlengraben, *m.* ⸗ mill brook
or ditch
Müller, *m.* — miller
Mund, *m.* (-e *or* ⸗er, *both rare*)
mouth
munter merry, cheerful
mürbe tender, soft, brittle
murmeln, *intr.* murmur
Musik, *f.* music
Mut, *m.* courage, spirit
Mutter, *f.* ⸗ mother
Mütze, *f.* -n cap
Myrte, *f.* -n myrtle

N

Nachforschung, *f.* -en searching
out, exploring
nach⸗gehen, *intr.* go after, follow
nach⸗gellen, *intr.* echo *or* reverberate shrilly
Nachmittag, *m.* -e afternoon
nach⸗sehen, a, e; ie, *intr.* follow

a person with one's gaze (*with dat.*)

nach=tönen, *intr.* keep on sounding, reverberate *or* echo

Nacht, *f.* ⸚e night

nächtens at night

Nachtigall, *f.* -en nightingale

nächtlich nightly, nocturnal

nackend ⎱ naked
nackt ⎰

Nacken, *m.* — neck

nahe near, close to; **nah an** close to

Nähe, *f.* nearness, presence

nahen, *refl.* approach, draw near

nähen, *tr.* sew

Nahrung, *f.* -en food

Name, *m.* -ns, -n name

naß wet, moist

Natter, *f.* -n viper, adder

Natur, *f.* -en nature

Nebel, *m.* — fog, mist

necken, *tr.* tease; **neckend** playful

nehmen, a, omm; imm, *tr.* take

neidisch envious

neigen, *tr. and refl.* bow, bend

Nest, *n.* -er nest

netzen, *tr.* wet, moisten, wash

neu new

Neujahr, *n.* New Year

nicken, *intr.* nod

nie never

nieder, *sep. pref.* down, downward

nieder=brechen, ā, o; i, *intr.* plunge down

Niederländer, *m.* — Dutchman; Dutch Master (*i.e.*, painter)

nieder=liegen, a, e, *for* **darnieder=liegen**, *intr.* lie prostrate

nieder=steigen, ie, ie *intr.* descend

nimmer never, nevermore

nimmermehr nevermore

nimmersatt insatiable

nirgends nowhere

Nixe, *f.* -n nymph

Nord(en), *m.* north

Nordlicht, *n.* -er northern lights

Normann(e), *m.* -en Norman

Not, *f.* ⸚e dire need, distress

nun now

O

obgleich although

obschon even if, although

öde desolate, waste

offen open

öffnen, *tr. and refl.* open

Öffnung, *f.* -en opening

Ohr, *n.* -s, -en ear

Oktober, *m.* October

Opfer, *n.* — sacrifice

Orakel, *n.* — oracle; —**spruch** *m.* ⸚e utterance of the oracle

Orange, *f.* -n orange

Ort, *m.* -e *and* ⸚er place, spot

Ost(en), *m.* east

P

Paar, *n.* -e pair, couple

Page, *m.* -n page

Palast, *m.* ⸚e palace

Palme, *f.* -n palm (tree)

Panier, *n.* -e banner

Pantoffel, *m.* -s, -(n) slipper

Panzer, *m.* — coat of mail

passen, *intr.* watch, wait for

passieren, *intr.* (f) happen

Pauke, *f.* -n kettle drum; —**nkrach**, *m.* rattle of drums

Pein, *f.* pain, torment

peitschen, *tr.* lash, whip

Perserschah, *m.* Shah of Persia

Pfad, *m.* -e path
pfeifen, iff, iff, *tr.* whistle
Pfeil, *m.* -e arrow
Pferd, *n.* -e horse
Pfingsten, *f. pl.* Pentecost
pflanzen, *tr.* plant
Pflug, *m.* ‑e plow
Pfühl, *m., n.* -e pillow, bolster, cushion
Piccolo, *f.* piccolo (*a small shrill flute*)
picken, *tr. and intr.* tick (*of a watch*)
Pinsel, *m.* — painter's brush
plätschern, *intr.* ripple, splash
plötzlich suddenly
pochen, *intr.* beat, knock
Pokal, *m.* -e goblet
Port, *m.* -e port
Post, *f.* -en mail, mail coach
Posthorn, *n.* ‑er postman's horn
Postillion, *m.* -e postilion
Pracht, *f.* splendor
prächtig splendid, magnificent
Preis, *m.* -e prize; the best of all
preisen, ie, ie, *tr.* praise
pressen, *tr.* press, choke
Puk, *m.* Puck
pulsen, *intr.* pulse
Pulver, *n.* — powder
Pupille, *f.* -n pupil (*of the eye*)

Q

Qual, *f.* -en torment, torture, pain
quälen, *tr.* torment, torture
Qualm, *m.* dense smoke *or* vapor
qualmen, *intr.* rise in fumes, give forth smoke

Quartier, *n.* -e quarters
Quell, *m.* (Quelle *f.*) -en spring, fountain
quellen, *intr.* well, flow
querfeldein through the fields

R

Rache, *f.* revenge, vengeance
rächen (*archaic* o, o), *tr. and refl.* revenge, avenge
Rächer, *m.* — avenger
Rad, *n.* ‑er wheel
ragen, *intr.* tower, loom up
Rand, *m.* ‑er edge, rim
rasch quick, fast
rascheln, *intr.* rustle
rasen, *intr.* rage
Rasen, *m.* — greensward, turf
rasten, *intr.* rest
raten, ie, a; ä *tr.* counsel
rauben, *tr.; jemandem etwas* — rob *or* deprive a person of a thing
Räuber, *m.* — robber
rauh rough, rude
Raum, *m.* ‑e space, realm, room, place
rauschen, *intr.* roar, rustle; *leis rauschend* softly rustling *or* murmuring
Rebe, *f.* -n grape
Rechnung, *f.* -en bill, account
recht right; true, real
rege active
regen, *refl.* move, stir
Regen, *m.* rain
Regenbogen, *m.* — rainbow
regungslos motionless
Reh, *n.* -e roe, deer
reich rich
Reich, *n.* -e empire, realm
reichen, *tr.* reach; give

reifen, *tr. and intr.* ripen

Reigen, *m.* — a round dance

Reihe, *f.* –n row

reihen, *tr. and refl.* arrange; join in row *or* line

Reihen, *m.* = Reigen

rein clean, pure

Reise, *f.* –n journey

reisen, *intr.* travel, journey

reißen, ĭ, ĭ, *tr.* tear, pull, draw

reiten, itt, itt, *intr.* ride

Reiter, *m.* — rider, horseman

Reitersmann, *m., pl.* —leute *poet.* for Reiter

reizen, *tr.* allure, attract, charm

rennen, rannte, gerannt, *intr.* run, race

Requiem, *n.* requiem

Rest, *m.* –e remnant

retten, *tr.* rescue, save

Retter, *m.* — rescuer

Reue, *f.* repentance, remorse

Revier, *n.* –e territory, ground

Rhein, *m.* Rhine

richten, *tr.* judge; das Wort an jemanden — address somebody

riechen, ŏ, ŏ, *tr.* scent, smell, sniff

Riese, *m.* –n giant

riesengroß of gigantic size

Riesengröße, *f.* –n giant size

riesenhaft gigantic

Riesenmaß, *n.* –e giant stature *or* size

Ring, *m.* –e ring, circle

Ringelreihen, *m.* — round dance

ringen, a, u, *tr.* struggle, fight

rings, rings herum round about, on all sides

rinnen, a, o, *intr.* flow, stream

Rippe, *f.* –n rib

rippendürr skinny, gaunt (*so thin that the ribs protrude*)

Ritter, *m.* — knight

Ritterschaft, *f.* knighthood

röcheln, *intr.* rattle in one's throat, breathe the last gasp

Rock, *m.* ⁻e coat

Rocken, *m.* — distaff

Rohr, *n.* –e reed, cane; tube, pipe (*hence* smokestack, chimney)

rollen, *tr. and intr.* roll

Römer, *m.* — Roman

römisch Roman

Rose, *f.* –n rose

Rosenband, *n.* ⁻er wreath *or* garland of roses

rosenfarben rose-colored

Rosenkranz, *m.* ⁻e rosary

Roß, *n.* –sse steed

rot red

Rotonde, *f.* –n rotunda

rücken, *tr. and intr.* move

rückwärts backward

Ruder, *n.* — oar

rudern, *intr. and tr.* row

Rudertakt, *m.* rhythm of the oars

rufen, ie, u, *tr. and intr.* call, cry, shout

Rufer, *m.* — caller

Ruhe, *f.* rest, quiet; in Ruh' lassen leave alone *or* undisturbed

ruhen, *intr.* rest

Ruhestätte, *f.* –n resting place

ruhig calm, quiet

Ruhm, *m.* fame, glory

Ruhmesmorgen, *m.* morning (*i.e.*, beginning) of fame

rühren, *tr.* stir, move; touch; wield

rund round

Runb, *n.* -e round

Runbe, *f.* -n circle; tofenbe Runbe boisterous circle of the dance

Rune, *f.* -n runic letter

Runenftein, *m.* -e rune stone

Rußlanb, *n.* Russia

Rüftung, *f.* -en armor, coat of mail

S

Saal, *m.* ⸚e hall

Saat, *f.* -en seed, grain sown; young crop

Saatengrün, *n.* the green of young crops

Sache, *f.* -n matter, cause; meine — my affair

facht soft

fäen, *tr.* sow

Säer, *m.* — sower

Sage, *f.* -n myth, legend

fagen, *tr.* say

Saite, *f.* -n string (*of a musical instrument*)

famt (*prep. with dat.*) together with

Sand, *m.* sand

fanft gentle

Sang, *m.* song

Sänger, *m.* — singer

Sängertum, *n.* minstrelsy

Sattel, *m.* ⸚ saddle

fauber neat

faugen, o, o, *tr.* suck, drink in

Säule, *f.* -n pillar, column

Saum, *m.* ⸚e hem, edge, border

fäumen, *tr.* hem, fringe

fäufeln, *intr.* rustle

faufen, *intr.* rush, roar, whiz

Schacht, *m.* -e gorge, ravine; shaft (*in a mine*)

fchabe: es ift — it is a pity; ewig — great pity

Schäfer, *m.* — shepherd

fchaffen, ü, a, *tr.* create, bring forth; *intr. and tr. weak verb* work, do

Schale, *f.* -n cup, bowl; scale (*of a balance*); in gleichen Schalen in equal scales

fchallen, *weak and* o, o, sound, resound

Schalmei, *f.* -en reed pipe, shawm

Schar, *f.* -en flock, crowd

Schärpe, *f.* -n sash, scarf

Schatten, *m.* — shadow, shade

fchattenfrei free from shade, unshaded

Schauber, *m.* — shudder, thrill of awe

fchauen, *tr. and intr.* look, gaze, see, behold

Schauer, *m.* — thrill of awe, shudder

fchauerlich causing a shudder, horrible

fchauern, *intr.* shudder

Schaugerüfte, *n.* — stage, platform

fchäumen, *intr.* foam

fchaurig horrible

Schaufpiel, *n.* -e drama

Scheibe, *f.* -n line of separation

fcheiben, ie, ie, *tr. and intr.* separate, part, leave

Scheibetag, *m.* -e day of parting

Scheibewand, *f.* ⸚e partition

Schein, *m.* -e light, glow

fcheinen, ie, ie, *intr.* shine, gleam; seem

Scheitel, *m.* — crown *or* top of the head

Schelle, *f.* -n bell

Schellenträger, *m.* — crescent player (*the crescent* Schellenbaum, *m.,* = *a crescent-shaped instrument with a series of bells that are struck with a hammer*)

Schelm, *m.* -e rogue, rascal

Schemen, *m.* — phantom, shadow

schenken, *tr.* present, give

scheren, *tr.* vex, tease; was schert mich das? what does that matter to me *or* concern me?

scheu shy, timid, timorous

scheuchen, *tr.* shy *or* frighten away

Scheuer, *f.* -n barn, granary

schicken, *tr.* send

Schicksal, *n.* -e fate, destiny

schier sheer

schießen, ö, ö, *tr. and intr.* shoot; *intr.* (= sich schnell bewegen) shoot *or* dash along; zur Erde — to plunge to earth

Schiff, *n.* -e ship

schiffen, *intr.* travel by ship, sail

Schiffer, *m.* — sailor, boatman

Schild, *m.* -e shield

Schilderklang, *m.* ringing *or* clanking of shields

Schildwache, *f.* -n sentinel, guard

Schilf, *n.* sedge

schilfig covered with sedge

schimmern, *intr.* glisten, gleam

schirmen, *tr.* protect, shield

Schlaf, *m.* sleep

Schläfe, *f.* -n temple

schlafen, ie, a; ä, *intr.* sleep

schläfrig sleepy

Schlag, *m.* -e blow, stroke

schlagen, u, a; ä, *tr.* beat, strike; die Saiten — strike the

chords; den Mantel um jemanden — throw the mantle around someone; *intr.* beat; (*of birds*) sing

Schlange, *f.* -n snake

schlank slender

schleichen, i, i, *intr.* steal, slip *or* creep along

Schleier, *m.* — veil

Schleppe, *f.* -n train (*of a dress*)

schleppen, *tr.* drag

schleudern, *tr.* hurl

schließen, ö, ö, *tr.* close

schließlich finally

Schlinge, *f.* -n snare, sling

schlingen, a, u, *tr.* wind, circle

Schloß, *n.* -ßer castle

Schlucht, *f.* -en ravine

Schlummer, *m.* slumber

Schlummerer, *m.* — slumberer

schlummerlos slumberless

schlummern, *intr.* slumber

Schmach, *f.* disgrace

schmal narrow

Schmaus, *m.* -e feast, banquet

schmeicheln, *intr.* (*with dat.*) flatter

Schmerz, *m.* -es, -en pain

schmerzenlos painless

Schmetterling, *m.* -e butterfly

Schmied, *m.* -e smith

Schmiede, *f.* -n smithy

schmuck trim, handsome

schmücken, *tr.* adorn, deck

schnarchen, *intr.* snore

Schnee, *m.* snow

schneiden, itt, itt, *tr.* cut

schneien, *intr.* snow

schnell quick

Schnitter, *m.* — reaper

schnöde mean, despicable

schnüren, *tr.* lace

Scholle, *f.* -n clod

ſchön beautiful, fair

Schönheit, f. –en beauty

Schrank, m. ⸗e cupboard, press, case

Schrecken, m. — terror

ſchreckenbleich pale with terror

Schrei, m. –e cry, scream

ſchreiben, ie, ie, tr. write

ſchreien, ie, ie, tr. and intr. scream, shout, cry

Schrein, m. –e shrine

ſchreiten, itt, itt, intr. step, stride; ihm zur Seite — walk at his side; zum Sturme — proceed to attack

Schrift, f. –en writing

Schritt, m. –e step, pace

ſchrittweiſe step by step

Schuld, f. –en guilt, debt

ſchuldbewußt conscious of guilt

ſchuldig guilty

Schulter, f. –n shoulder

Schuppe, f. –n scale

Schuppenkette, f. –n scale chain

ſchüren, tr. stir up; das Feuer — poke the fire

Schuß, m. ⸗ſſe shot; ein — fällt a shot is heard

Schutt, m. rubble, debris

Schutz, m. protection

ſchützen, tr. protect, shield

ſchwach weak, feeble

Schwager, m. ⸗ brother-in-law; coachman (corruption of chevalier)

Schwalbe, f. –n swallow

Schwan, m. ⸗e swan

ſchwanken, intr. waver, vacillate

Schwarm, m. ⸗e swarm

ſchwarz black

ſchwärzlich blackish

ſchwatzen, tr. and intr. chatter, chat, gossip

ſchweben, intr. hover

Schweif, m. –e tail (as of a horse or of a peacock); train (of a garment)

ſchweifen, intr. roam, rove; tr. curve, slope

ſchweigen, ie, ie, intr. be silent; (as a noun = silence)

Schweizerland, n. (= die Schweiz) Switzerland

Schwelle, f. –n threshold

ſchwellen, o, o; i, intr. swell, rise; manch Herze ſchwoll many a heart beat high; der Klang zum Ohre ſchwoll the sound surged in upon the ear

ſchwenken, tr. swing, shake, flourish

ſchwer heavy; grievous

Schwert, n. –er sword

Schweſter, f. –n sister

ſchwimmen, a, o, intr. swim

ſchwindeln, intr. be dizzy; ſchwindelnde Höhen dizzying heights

ſchwinden, a, u, intr. dwindle, vanish, disappear

Schwinge, f. –n pinion, wing

ſchwingen, a, u, tr. and intr. swing; ſich aufs Pferd — mount; das Rad — turn the wheel

ſchwirren, intr. whir

ſchwören, o, o, tr. swear, vow

ſchwül sultry

Schwüle, f. sultry heat, sultriness

Schwung, m. –e swing

See, m. –s, –n lake

See, f. –n sea, ocean; zur — on the sea

Seele, f. –n soul

ſegeln, intr. sail

Segen, *m.* — blessing

segnen, *tr.* bless

sehen, a, e; ie, *tr. and intr.* see

Sehnsucht, *f.* longing, yearning

sehnsuchtsvoll full of longing

Seide, *f.* -n silk

seiden silk, silken

seitab apart, off to one side

Seite, *f.* -n side

selig blessed, blissful

Seligkeit, *f.* -en bliss, *esp.* heavenly bliss

seltsam strange

senden, sandte, gesandt, *tr.* send

senken, *tr.* cause to sink, lower; mit gesenktem Haupte with bowed head

Sense, *f.* -n scythe

setzen, *tr.* set, place, put

seufzen, *intr.* sigh

Seufzer, *m.* — sigh

Sichel, *f.* -n sickle

sicher firm, safe

Sieg, *m.* -e victory

Silber, *n.* silver

silbern silver, silvery

singen, a, u, *tr. and intr.* sing

sinken, a, u, *intr.* sink, descend; *(of eyes)* close

Sinn, *m.* -e sense, mind, spirit, thought, intent

sinnen, a, o, *tr. and intr.* think, ponder, meditate

Sippschaft, *f.* -en kin, kinfolk

Sitte, *f.* -n custom

Sitz, *m.* -e seat

sitzen, saß, gesessen, *intr.* sit

Sklave, *m.* -n slave

sobald, *conj.* as soon as

sogar, *adv.* even

sogleich at once, immediately

Sohle, *f.* -n sole; bottom of a valley

Sohn, *m.* ⸚e son

Soldat, *m.* -en soldier

Sommer, *m.* — summer

sonderbar strange, unusual

Sonne, *f.* -n sun

Sonnenregen, *m.* rain that falls during sunshine, "sun shower"

Sonnenschein, *m.* sunshine

Sonntag, *m.* -e Sunday, Sabbath

sonst otherwise; besides; — nichts naught else

Sorge, *f.* -n care

sorgen, *intr.* care for, take care of

Span, *m.* ⸚e chip, splinter

Spange, *f.* -n buckle, clasp; bracelet

spannen, *tr.* stretch, bend; das Gezelt — pitch the tent

sparen, *tr.* save

spät late

Spätboot, *n.* -e *or* —böte late evening boat

Spaten, *m.* — spade

Speer, *m.* -e spear

Speise, *f.* -n food

speisen, *tr. and intr.* eat; feast on

sperren, *tr.* bar, block

spiegeln, *tr.* mirror, reflect

Spiel, *n.* -e play, game; mit etwas sein — treiben make sport of a thing

spielen, *tr. and intr.* play

Spielmann, *m., pl.* —leute minstrel

spinnen, a, o, *tr.* spin

Splitter, *m.* — splinter, fragment, shred

Sporn, *m.* -s, Sporen spur; einem Pferde die Sporen geben put spurs to a horse

Spott, *m.* mockery, jest

spotten, *intr.* mock, jeer, deride

sprechen, ā, o; i, *tr. and intr.* speak, say

sprengen, *intr.* gallop

sprießen, ŏ, ŏ, *intr.* sprout

Springbrunn, *m.* –s, –en fountain

springen, a, u, *intr.* spring, leap, jump; (*of sparks*) fly; (*of a brook*) gush *or* play

Spruch, *m.* ⸚e verse, motto

Sprung, *m.* ⸚e leap, jump, bound

Spur, *f.* –en trace, track, clue

spüren, *intr.* trace, track; *tr.* notice, feel

Stab, *m.* ⸚e staff; bar

Stadt, *f.* ⸚e city, town

Staffelei, *f.* –en easel

Stamm, *m.* ⸚e tribe

stampfen, *tr. and intr.* stamp

Stange, *f.* –n beam, pole, stalk

Stapfe, *f.* –n footstep, footprint

stark strong

starr rigid, motionless

starren, *intr.* stare

stattlich stately, splendid

Staub, *m.* dust

stäuben, *intr.* fly like dust, spray

Staubgewand, *n.* ⸚er garb of dust

staunen, *intr.* marvel, wonder

stechen, ā, o; i, *tr.* sting, prick; stab, pierce

stecken, *intr.* be, hide; *tr.* stick, place, erect

Steg, *m.* –e path; narrow wooden bridge

stehen, stand, gestanden *intr.* stand

stehlen, a, o; ie, *tr.* steal

steigen, ie, ie, *intr.* rise, ascend

steil steep

Stein, *m.* –e stone, rock

steinern (of) stone

sterben, a, o; i, *intr.* die

sterblich mortal

Stern, *m.* –e star

Sternenblume, *f.* –n small wild aster (*alpine*)

sternenwärts starward

Sternenzeit, *f.* –en time of the stars (*i.e.*, night)

sternklar starry clear

stets always

Steuer, *n.* — rudder

Steurer, *m.* — helmsman

still silent, still

Stille, *f.* silence

stillen, *tr.* hush, assuage

Stimme, *f.* –n voice

Stirn(e), *f.* –n brow, forehead

stöhnen, *intr.* groan

stolz proud

Stolz, *m.* pride

stören, *tr.* disturb

Stoß, *m.* ⸚e thrust, blow

stoßen, ie, o; ö, *tr.* thrust, push

Strahl, *m.* –s, –en beam *or* ray (*of light*); jet *or* stream (*of water*)

strahlen, *intr.* beam, shine

Strahlenspuren, *pl.* traces of radiance

stramm sturdy

Strand, *m.* –e strand

Straße, *f.* –n street

Straßentreiben, *n.* bustle *or* stir of life on the streets

Strauch, *m.* ⸚er bush

Strauß, *m.* ⸚e bouquet

streben, *intr.* strive

strecken, *tr.* stretch

Streich, *m.* –e blow, stroke

ftreid)eln, *tr.* caress, stroke

ftreid)en, ĭ, ĭ, *tr.* stroke; *intr.*
pass *or* roam along

Streif, *m.* -e = Streifen, *m.* -en
strip

ftreifen, *tr.* pass along, brush

Streit, *m.* -e battle, combat

ftreng severe, stern

ftreuen, *tr.* strew (burd)einander
helter-skelter)

Strid), *m.* -e stroke (*as with a
pen or brush*)

Strol), *n.* straw

Strom, *m.* ⁼e stream, river

ftrömen, *intr.* stream

ftroßen, *intr.* swell, be full to
bursting

Stube, *f.* -n room, chamber

Stüd, *n.* -e piece, part

Stufe, *f.* -n step (*of a stairway*);
tier (*of seats*)

ftufenweife by steps

ftumm mute, silent, dumb

Stunde, *f.* -n hour

Sturm, *m.* ⁼e storm; attack

ftürmen, *intr.* storm, rage

Sturmglode, *f.* -n tocsin

Sturz, *m.* ⁼e plunge, fall

ftürzen, *intr.* plunge, fall

Stüße, *f.* -n support, prop

ftußen, *intr.* start back, stop
short, startle

fud)en, *tr.* seek, look for

Süden, *m.* south

füljnen, *tr.* atone, expiate

Sultan, *m.* -e Sultan

Summe, *f.* -n sum

fummen, *intr.* hum, buzz

Sünde, *f.* -n sin

Sünder, *m.* — sinner

füß sweet

Syringe, *f.* -n lilac

Szene, *f.* -n scene

T

Tag, *m.* -e day

täglid) daily

Tagwerf, *n.* -e daily labor, day's
work

Tal, *n.* ⁼er valley

Tanne, *f.* -n evergreen, pine

Tanz, *m.* ⁼e dance

tanzen, *intr.* dance

Tanzplan, *m.* dance floor;
(Plan, *m.* glade)

tapfer brave

Taffe, *f.* -n cup

taften, *intr.* grope, feel about

Tat, *f.* -en deed

Täter, *m.* — doer

Tau, *m.* dew

taud)en, *tr.* dip, plunge, im-
merse; *intr.* dive

taufd)en, *tr.* exchange

täufd)en, *tr.* deceive

Tee, *m.* tea

Teid), *m.* -e pond

teilen, *tr.* share, apportion

Tempel, *m.* — temple

teuer dear

Theater, *n.* — theater

Thron, *m.* -e, (-en) throne

thronen, *intr.* be enthroned

Thronenflitter, *m.* — royal
pomp

tief deep

Tiefe, *f.* -n depth

Tod)ter, *f.* ⁼ daughter

Tod, *m.* -e death

Todesglut, *f.* -en deadly glow

Todeskampf, *m.* ⁼e death struggle

Todesritt, *m.* ride of death

toll mad

Ton, *m.* ⁼e tone

tönen, *intr.* sound, resound, ring

Tor, *n.* -e gate, portal
töricht foolish
tofen, *intr.* rage, roar
tot dead
Totenbahre, *f.* -n bier
Totenschrein, *m.* -e shrine for
the dead (*i.e.*, coffin)
Totenstille, *f.* dead silence
traben, *intr.* trot
Tracht, *f.* -en garb, costume
träge idle, lazy
tragen, u, a; ä, *tr.* carry, bear
Träne, *f.* -n tear
trauen, *intr.* (*with dat.*) trust
Trauer, *f.* mourning, sadness
trauern, *intr.* mourn
traulich cozy
Traum, *m.* ⸚e dream
träumen, *tr. and intr.* dream
(ich träume *or* mir träumt)
träumerisch dreamy
Traumesflug, *m.* flight *or* passing of a dream
traurig sad
traut dear, beloved, sweetly
familiar
treffen, ā, o; i, *tr.* strike, hit
treiben, ie, ie, drive; carry on
(*as a noun* = bustle, stir,
contending)
trennen, *tr.* separate
treten, a, e; itt, *intr.* step; ins
Glied — step into line
treu faithful
Treue, *f.* faithfulness, troth
treulos faithless
Tribunal, *n.* -e tribunal
Trieb, *m.* -e impulse, impetus
trinken, a, u, *tr. and intr.* drink
Tritt, *m.* -e step
Triumph, *m.* -e triumph
trocknen, *tr. and intr.* dry
Trommel, *f.* -n drum

tropfen, *intr.* drip
Tropfen, *m.* — drop
Trost, *m.* consolation
Trostgebärde, *f.* consoling ges-
ture
trostlos disconsolate
trotzen, *intr.* (*with dat.*) defy
trotzig defiant, bold
trübe sad, melancholy
Trug, *m.* deception, delusion
Truhe, *f.* -n chest, trunk
Trümmer, *n. pl.* ruins
Trunk, *m.* drink, potion
Tuba, *f.* -s *and* Tuben tuba
tun, a, a; *tr.* do
Tür, *f.* -en door
Türkentrommel, *f.* -n kettle-
drum
Turm, *m.* ⸚e tower
türmen, *intr.* tower; *tr.* pile up

U

üben, *tr. and refl.* practise, exer-
cise; use, give play to, exert
überdies moreover, besides
Überfluß, *m.* abundance, pro-
fusion
überfluten, *tr.* inundate, cover
(*as with a flood*)
Übergang, *m.* ⸚e crossing, tran-
sition
überlassen, ie, a; ä, *tr.* leave to
überschallen, *tr.* drown out, out-
sound
überschlagen, u, a; ä, *tr.* cover
überschütten, *tr.* pour over,
cover
überspülen, *tr.* overflood, inundate
übersteigen, ie, ie, *tr.* surmount
überwältigen, *tr.* conquer, overcome

überwehen, *tr.* blow over

Ufer, *n.* — bank, shore

Uhrgehäuse, *n.* — outer case of a clock

um=bringen, brachte, gebracht, *tr.* rob of life, put to death

umfangen, i, a; ä, *tr.* embrace, surround, enclose

umflechten, o, o; i, *tr.* entwine, encircle (*cf.* flechten)

umflimmern, *tr.* surround with flickering light

umflügeln, *tr.* fly around, encircle in flight

umgeben, a, e; i, *tr.* surround

um=gürten, *tr.* gird *or* buckle on

umhallen, *tr.* surround with sound

umher=geisten, *intr.* move about like ghosts *or* phantoms

umhüllen, *tr.* enwrap, envelop

umrahmen, *tr.* frame

umsausen, *tr.* roar around; whiz around

umsonst in vain

umwandeln, *tr.* encircle in wandering

umwinden, a, u, *tr.* wind about, encircle, entwine

umwogen, *tr.* flow around, encircle (*as waves do*)

unaufgefunden unfound, undiscovered

unbeweint unmourned

unbewußt unconscious

unchristlich unchristian

unendlich infinite, endless

unerforschlich inscrutable

unergründet unfathomed

unergründlich unfathomable

unerreichlich unattainable

unfreiwillig involuntary

ungebrochen unbroken

ungeduldig impatient

Ungeheuer, *n.* — monster

ungehört unheard

ungesehen unseen

ungestüm impetuous

ungeteilt undivided

ungeweiht unhallowed

ungewiß uncertain

unmutig vexed, angry

unscheinbar plain, not resplendent

unsicher unsafe, uncertain

unsichtbar invisible

Unsterblichkeit, *f.* -en immortality

unterbrechen, ā, o; i, *tr.* interrupt

unter=gehen, ging, gegangen, *intr.* go down; perish; (*of the sun*) set

Unterlaß, *m.*; *occurs only in* ohne Unterlaß incessantly

unterscheiden, ie, ie, *tr.* distinguish

unverbunden not bandaged

unverrückt undisturbed, not moved out of place

unversehens unexpectedly

unverstellt undisguised, unhidden

unverwüstlich indestructible (verwüsten, *tr.* = lay waste, devastate)

unzählig beyond number, numberless

üppig luxuriant, rich

uralt very old, ancient, primeval

Urne, *f.* -n urn

V

Vater, *m.* ⸗ father

Vaterland, *n.* ⸗er fatherland

Väterſaal, *m.* -ſäle ancestral hall

Veilchen, *n.* — violet

verbeißen, ĭ, ĭ, *tr.* suppress, stifle

verbergen, a, o; i, *tr.* hide, conceal

verbieten, o, o, *tr.* forbid

verbleichen, ĭ, ĭ, *intr.* fade, turn pale

verbringen, verbrachte, verbracht, *tr.* spend, pass

verderben, a, o; i, *intr.* perish

Verderben, *n.* destruction, ruin

verdienen, *tr.* deserve, merit

verdorren, *intr.* wither, dry up

verdrängen, *tr.* push aside, crowd out, displace

verdrießen, ŏ, ŏ, *tr.* vex, grieve

verdunkeln, *tr.* darken

vereinen, *tr.* unite

verengen, *tr.* narrow, contract, compress

Verfall, *m.* ruin

verfliegen, o, o, *intr.* fly away, vanish

verfließen, ŏ, ŏ, *intr.* flow off *or* away; (*of time*) pass by

verführen, *tr.* lead astray, seduce

vergehen, verging, vergangen, *intr.* vanish, pass away

vergeſſen, ā, e; i, *tr.* forget (*in poetry sometimes with gen.*)

vergleichen, ĭ, ĭ, *tr.* compare

vergnügt happy, contented

vergolden, *tr.* gild; den grauen Tag — turn the gray day into gold

vergönnen, *tr.* grant, allow

verhallen, *intr.* (*of sound*) vanish, die away

verhalten, ie, a; ä, *tr.* suppress, restrain

verhängt (*of reins*) slackened; mit verhängtem Zügel at full speed

verhauchen, *tr.* breathe out, expire

verhüllen, *tr.* cover, veil, hide

verhundertfältigen, *tr.* multiply a hundredfold

verirren, *intr. and refl.* go astray, err

verklingen, a, u, *intr.* (*of sound*) die away, vanish

verkünden, *tr.* announce, make known

verlangen, *tr.* demand; mich verlangt nach etwas I long for something

Verlangen, *n.* desire, longing

verlaſſen, ie, a; ä, *tr.* leave, forsake

verleihen, ie, ie, *tr.* grant, bestow upon

verlernen unlearn, forget

verliebt in love, enamored, lovelorn

verlieren, o, o, *tr.* lose

verlocken, *tr.* entice

vermählen, *tr.* give in marriage; *refl.* marry, wed (mit jemand)

vermeinen, *intr.* think, believe

vermögen, vermochte, vermocht (*inflected like* mögen) *tr.* (*with* zu *and infinitive*) be able (to do a thing)

vernehmen, a, omm; imm, *tr.* become aware of, perceive, hear

veröden, *intr.* become waste *or* desolate; *tr.* lay waste *or* devastate

verraten, ie, a; ä, *tr.* betray

verrauſchen, *intr.* rush away, hurry past, rustle *or* rush by verreifen, *intr.* go on a journey

verröcheln, *intr.* expire, breathe the death rattle

verrucht accursed, ruthless

verfagen, *tr.* refuse

verfammeln, *tr. and refl.* gather, collect

verfcharren, *tr.* bury (hurriedly *or* carelessly)

verfcheiden, ie, ie, *intr.* pass away, die

verfchlafen drowsy with sleep

verfchleiern, *tr.* veil

verfchließen, ŏ, ŏ, *tr.* close up

verfchlingen, a, u, *tr.* engulf, swallow up

verfchränken, *tr. and refl.* interlink; die Arme — fold one's arms

verfchweigen, ie, ie, *tr.* keep secret, conceal

verfchwenden, *tr.* lavish, give in abundance

verfchwinden, a, u, *intr.* disappear

verfehren, *tr.* injure, damage, defile

verfenken, *tr.* sink, bury

verfetzen, *tr.* reply

verfiegen, *intr.* run dry, dry up

verfinken, a, u, *intr.* sink down, go to the bottom; in Leid verfunken buried *or* lost in sorrow

verföhnen, *tr.* reconcile; propitiate, appease

verfpäten, *tr. and refl.* make late, delay

verfprechen, ā, o; i, *tr.* promise

verfpüren, *tr.* notice, feel

Verständnis, *n.* understanding

verständnisfinnig with deep understanding

verfteint covered with stones

verfterben, a, o, *intr.* die out

verftohlen stealthy, in secret

verftören, *tr.* disturb, upset, bewilder

verftreuen, *tr.* scatter, disperse

verftummen, *intr.* grow mute, become silent

verfuchen, *tr.* tempt

vertrauen, *tr.* entrust; vertraut confiding, trusting

verwacht weary with waking

verwaifen, *intr.* become an orphan; verwaift orphaned

verwehen, *tr.* (*of the wind*) blow *or* drive away; *intr.* be blown away, scatter

verwildern, *intr.* grow wild

verwirren, *tr.* confuse; *p.p.*, verworren confused

verwundert astonished

verzehren, *tr.* consume

viel much

vielleicht perhaps

Viererzug, *m.* ⸗e team of four

Vogel, *m.* ⸗ bird

vogelfprachekund understanding the language of the birds

Volk, *n.* ⸗er people, folk

voll full

vollenden, *tr.* complete, accomplish

Vollkommenheit, *f.* -en perfection

Vollmond, *m.* -e full moon

voran before, at the head

vorbei gone, past, by

vorbei=fliegen, o, o, *intr.* fly by

Vorhang, *m.* ⸗e curtain

vor=klagen, *tr.* lament about

vor=kommen, ā, o, *intr.* seem, appear

vor=fprechen, ā, o; i, *tr.* pronounce a word before a person; ſich etwas — say a thing to oneself

vorüber past

vorüber=gehen, ging, gegangen, *intr.* go past *or* by, pass

vorwärts ahead, forward

W

wach awake

wachen, *intr.* be awake

wachſen, u, a; ä, *intr.* grow

Wächter, *m.* — watchman, guard

Wachtgebell, *n.* watch bark (*of dogs*)

wacker brave, good

Wage, *f.* -n balance, pair of scales

wagen, *tr.* dare, venture

Wagen, *m.* — wagon, chariot

wählen, *tr.* choose, elect

wahrhaftig indeed, in truth

Wahrheit, *f.* -en truth

wahrlich forsooth, indeed

Wald, *m.* ⁻er forest

Waldesnacht, *f.* ⁻e forest gloom

wallen, *intr.* wander, journey; wave, flutter, undulate

walten, *intr.* rule, hold sway

wälzen, *tr.* roll; *refl.* toss

Wand, *f.* ⁻e wall

Wandel, *m.* journeying, passing by; change

wandeln, *intr.* wander, journey

Wanderblick, *m.* -e wandering glance (*i.e.*, glance of a wanderer)

Wanderer, *m.* — wanderer

Wandergans, *f.* ⁻e wild goose

wandermüde tired of wandering

wandern, *intr.* wander

Wanderſang, *m.* ⁻e song of wandering

Wanderſchuh, *m.* -e wanderer's shoe

Wandersmann, *m. pl.* —leute *poet. for* Wanderer

Wange, *f.* -n cheek

wanken, *intr.* totter, waver, sway

warm warm

Wärme, *f.* warmth

wärmen, *tr.* warm

warnungsvoll full of warning

warten, *intr.* wait; *tr.* wait upon, serve

Wartfrau, *f.* -en nurse, female attendant

Waſſer, *n.* — water

Waſſerbahn, *f.* -en watery track, expanse of water

Waſſerſchacht, *m.* ⁻e shaft for water (*i.e.*, a well)

weben, o, o, *tr. and intr.* be astir, stir, move

wechſeln, *intr.* change

wecken, *tr.* awaken

weg away

Weg, *m.* -e way, path, road

weg=reißen, i, i, *tr.* tear away

weh woe; — dir woe to thee; — tun pain, hurt

wehen, *intr.* blow, be wafted

Wehmut, *f.* melancholy, sadness

wehren, *tr.* ward off (etwas von jemandem); *refl.* defend oneself, resist

Weib, *n.* -er woman; wife

weich soft

weichen, i, i, *intr.* give way, make room

Weide, *f.* -en willow

weiden, *intr.* graze; *tr.* drive to pasture; (*fig.*) feast

Weiher, *m.* — pond

Weihnachten, *pl.* (**Weihnacht** *f.*) Christmas

Weile, *f.* while, a short space of time; über eine kleine — a little while later

weilen, *intr.* stay, tarry, linger

Wein, *m.* -e wine

weinen, *intr. and tr.* weep

Weise, *f.* -n melody, tune

weisen, ie, ie, *tr.* show, point out

Weiser, *m.* — hand (*on a clock*)

Weisheit, *f.* -en wisdom

weiß white

weit spacious, wide; far (off)

weiter (*comparative of* weit) farther, further, on

weither from afar

Weizen, *m.* wheat

welk withered

welken, *intr.* wither, fade

Welle, *f.* -n wave

Wellenschlagen, *n.* beating, surging *or* falling and rising of the waves

Welt, *f.* -en world

wenden, *reg. or* wandte, gewandt, *tr. and refl.* turn; sich wenden change

werfen, a, o; i, *tr.* throw, cast

Wert, *m.* -e value

wesen, *intr.* be, be alive

Wesen, *n.* — being, creature; nature, character

Wette, *f.* -n wager

Wetter, *n.* — weather

wichtig weighty, important

Widerhall, *m.* echo

Widmung, *f.* -en dedication

wieder again

wieder-kommen, ā, o, *intr.* come again, return

wieder-pflanzen, *tr.* plant again, replant

Wiege, *f.* -n cradle

wiegen, *tr. and refl.* rock, swing

wiegen, o, o, *tr.* weigh

Wiegenlied, *n.* -er cradle song, lullaby

wiehern, *intr.* neigh, whinny

Wiese, *f.* -n meadow

Wiesental, *n.* ⸗er meadow (*in a valley*), vale

wild wild

Wille, *m.* will

willig willing

willkommen welcome

Willkommen, *m.*, *n.* greeting, welcome

wimmeln, *intr.* swarm, be alive with

wimmern, *intr.* cry in pain, moan, whine

Wimper, *f.* -n eyelash

Wind, *m.* -e wind, breeze

Winde, *f.* -n morning glory, vine

windstill calm, becalmed

windverweht carried away by the wind

winken, *intr.* beckon

Winter, *m.* — winter

Winzer, *m.* — vintager, gatherer of grapes

Wipfel, *m.* — treetop

Wirbel, *m.* — whirl, eddy

wirren, *tr.* confuse, entangle

Wirt, *m.* -e host, landlord

wirtlich hospitable

wispern, *intr.* make a soft sound, chirp

wissen, wußte, gewußt; weiß, *tr.* know

Wissen, *n.* knowledge

wittern, *tr.* scent, get wind of

Witz, *m.* -e wit, craft, cunning

Woche, f. -n week

Woge, f. -n wave, billow

wogen, intr. surge, wave

wohl well, indeed; perhaps, probably

wohlbekannt well known

wohlgegründet well founded

wohlig comfortable, snug and cozy

Wohllaut, m. euphony

wohnen, intr. dwell, live

Wolke, f. -n cloud

Wolkenbruch, m. ⸚e cloudburst, torrential downpour

Wolkenhülle, f. -n veil or covering of clouds

wolkenrein cloudless

wolkig cloudy

Wonne, f. -n bliss

wonniglich blissfully

Wort, n. -e and ⸚er word

wühlen, tr. burrow, dig up

Wunde, f. -n wound

Wunder, n. — wonder, miracle

wunderbar wondrous, wonderful

wunderschön wondrous fair, very beautiful

wundervoll wonderful, wondrous

Wunsch, m. ⸚e wish

wünschen, tr. wish

wurzeln, intr. take root, have root, grow

Wüste, f. -n desert

Wut, f. rage

wüten, intr. rage

3

Zahl, f. -en number

zählen, tr. count

Zähre, f. -n (poet.) tear

zart delicate

Zärtlichkeit, f. -en tender feeling, affection

Zauber, m. charm, spell

Zauberdunkel, n. magic darkness

zaubermächtig having magic power

Zaun, m. ⸚e hedge

Zecher, m. — drinker, carouser

Zehe, f. -n toe

Zeichen, n. — sign, token

zeigen, tr. show

Zeit, f. -en time, tide

Zeitvertreib, m. pastime

Zelt, n. -e tent, canopy

zentnerschwer very heavy, of grievous weight (Zentner, m. = hundredweight)

zerbrechen, a, o; i, tr. break

zerfließen, o, o, intr. dissolve; in eins — coalesce

zerreißen, i, i, tr. tear, rend

zerrinnen, a, o, intr. melt away, dissolve, vanish

zerschellen, tr. break, shatter; intr. be broken or shattered

zerschlagen, u, a; ä, tr. knock to pieces, shatter, batter to pieces

zerstampfen, tr. crush by stamping or trampling

zerstieben, o, o, intr. fly away, vanish

zerstören, tr. destroy

zertreten, a, e; itt, tr. crush under foot

zerwühlen, tr. claw (cf. wühlen)

zeugen, intr. testify, bear witness

zeugen, tr. beget

ziehen, o, o, intr. journey, pass, go; tr. pull, draw

Zier, *f.* decoration, grace

zierlich dainty, graceful

Zimmer, *n.* — room

Zinkenist, *m.* -en clarion player

zirpen, *intr.* chirp

Zither, *f.* -n zither

Zitrone, *f.* -n lemon

Zitterhand, *f.* ⸚e trembling hand

zittern, *intr.* tremble

Zone, *f.* -n zone

Zopf, *m.* ⸚e braid

zucken, *intr.* throb, quiver

zu=decken, *tr.* cover

Zufall, *m.* ⸚e chance

zu=fallen, ie, a; ä, *intr.* close

Zug, *m.* ⸚e feature; passage, passing

Zügel, *m.* — bridle, reins

zugleich simultaneous, at the same time

zünden, *tr.* light, kindle

zurück back, backward

zurück=schlagen, u, a; ä, *tr.* throw back, thrust back

zusammen together

zusammen=brechen, ā, o; i, *intr.* break down, collapse

Zusammenhang, *m.* ⸚e connection, interdependence

zusammen=nehmen, a, omm; imm, *tr. and refl.* gather (seine Kräfte — summon *or* collect one's strength)

zusammen=suchen, *tr.* gather up, collect

Zusatz, *m.* ⸚e addition, added stipulation

zu=senden, sandte, gesandt, *tr.* send toward

zuvor formerly

zuweilen at times

Zweifel, *m.* — doubt

Zweig, *m.* -e twig

zweigen, *intr.* put forth new branches, flourish

zweit: zu — for two, for both

Zwiegespräch, *n.* -e dialogue, conversation between two

zwingen, a, u, *tr.* force

zwitschern, *tr. and intr.* twitter, chirp

INDEX OF TITLES AND FIRST LINES

The figures refer to the numbers of the poems

Abendgefühl	94
Abendlandschaft	38
Abendlied	100
Abendwolke	127
Am grauen Strand, am grauen Meer	105
Am wolkenreinen Himmel geht	118
An das Vaterland	98
An ferne Berge schlug die Donnerkeulen	134
April	109
Auf Blut und Leichen, Schutt und Qualm	133
Auf dem See	3
Auf dem Teich, dem regungslosen	71
Auf eine holländische Landschaft	76
Auf eine Lampe	87
Auf Flügeln des Gesanges	50
Aufsteigt der Strahl und fallend gießt	119
Augen, meine lieben Fensterlein	100
Aus der Jugendzeit	45
Aus der Schiffsbank mach' ich meinen Pfühl	117
Befreit	144
Bei der Abendsonne wandern	126
Bemeßt den Schritt! Bemeßt den Schwung	121
Bitte	70
Bleib bei uns! wir haben den Tanzplan im Tal	37
Dämmernd liegt der Sommerabend	55
Dann	141
Das Glöcklein	128

Das Grab im Busento 66
Das ist der Tag des Herrn 22
Das ist die Drossel, die da schlägt 109
Das Kind 91
Das Licht 151
Das Schwert 27
Das tote Kind 116
Das verlassene Mägdlein 84
Das verschleierte Bild zu Sais 19
Das Wasser rauscht, das Wasser schwoll 13
Das zerbrochene Ringlein 41
Denk' es, o Seele 89
Der Arbeitsmann 139
Der Asra 65
Der du von dem Himmel bist 5
Der Eichwald 72
Der Einsiedel 148
Der Feuerreiter 83
Der Fischer 13
Der frohe Wandersmann 33
Der gute Kamerad 30
Der Hirt bläst seine Weise 38
Der Jäger Abschied 34
Der Knecht hat erstochen den edeln Herrn 28
Der König in Thule 12
Der Meister malt ein kleines zartes Bild 123
Der Nebel steigt, es fällt das Laub 102
Der offene Schrank 75
Der Panther 153
Der Postillion 73
Der römische Brunnen 119
Der Tod, das ist die kühle Nacht 57
Der Wirtin Töchterlein 29
Des Knaben Berglied 21
Des Menschen Seele 15
Des Sängers Fluch 32
Die armen Worte 152
Die Bank des Alten 129
Die Drei 74

Die du, über die Sterne weg. 93
Die Erblindende 154
Die Grenadiere 46
Die Kapelle 23
Die Kinder schreien Vivat hoch 110
Die Kraniche des Ibykus 18
Die Lerchen 20
Die linden Lüfte sind erwacht 25
Die Lotosblume ängstigt 51
Die Lüfte rasten auf der weiten Heide 77
Die Musik kommt. 130
Die Mutter lag im Totenschrein 91
Die Nacht. 39
Die Rache 28
Dies ist ein Herbsttag, wie ich keinen sah 97
Die Spange 147
Die Stadt. 105
Die stille Stadt. 140
Drei Reiter nach verlorner Schlacht 74
Droben stehet die Kapelle 23
Du bist wie eine Blume 49
Du mußt das Leben nicht verstehen 155
Du wirst nicht weinen 144

Eine Frühlingsnacht. 108
Ein Fichtenbaum steht einsam 52
Eingelegte Ruder 124
Ein gleiches 6
Ein Jüngling, den des Wissens heißer Durst 19
Ein Jüngling liebt ein Mädchen 54
Ein Tännlein grünet wo 89
Elfe 37
Elisabeth 111
Erinnerung 8
Er ist's 81
Erlkönig 14
Er steht an ihrem Pfühl 128
Es fällt ein Stern herunter 56
Es hat den Garten sich zum Freund gemacht 116

Es ist ein Brunnen 144
Es ragt ins Meer der Runenstein 63
Es schienen so golden die Sterne 40
Es schlug mein Herz, geschwind zu Pferde 1
Es stand in alten Zeiten ein Schloß so hoch und hehr 32
Es war, als hätt' der Himmel 44
Es war ein alter König 61
Es war ein König in Thule 12
Es ziehen die brausenden Wellen 62
Es zogen drei Bursche wohl über den Rhein 29
Ewig jung ist nur die Sonne 125

Frauenhand 112
Frieden 59
Friedlich bekämpfen 94
Frühe 42
Frühling läßt sein blaues Band 81
Frühlingsdämmerung 36
Frühlingsglaube 25
Früh, wann die Hähne krähn 84

Gebet 88, 93
Gefunden 9
Gelassen stieg die Nacht ans Land 79
Gesang der Geister über den Wassern 15
Gleichnis 145
Golden streift der Sommer 146
Grenzen der Menschheit 16

Harfenspieler 11
Heidenröslein 4
Herbst 78
Herbstbild 97
Herr, schicke, was du willt 88
Heute fanden meine Schritte mein vergeßnes Jugendtal 125
Hoch am Himmel stand die Sonne 59
Hochsommerlied 146
Hoffnung 7

Ich bin einmal in einem Tal gegangen 129
Ich bin vom Berg der Hirtenknab' 21
Ich ging im Walde 9
Ich hatte einst ein schönes Vaterland 64
Ich hatt' einen Kameraden 30
Ich möchte, wann ich sterbe, wie die lichten 69
Ich sah des Sommers letzte Rose stehn 96
Ich seh' sie noch, ihr Büchlein in der Hand 107
Ich stehe in Waldesschatten 35
Ich trat in einen heilig düstern 72
Ich und du 95
Ich wandre durch die stille Nacht 43
Ich weiß es wohl, kein klagend Wort 112
Ich weiß nicht, was soll es bedeuten 48
Ich wollte sie aus kühlem Eisen 147
Ihr tratet zu dem Herde 150
Im Nebel ruhet noch die Welt 80
Im Osten graut's, der Nebel fällt 42
Im Spätboot 117
Im Wasser wogt die Lilie 67
Im Weizenfeld, in Korn und Mohn 131
Im Zimmer drinnen ist's so schwül 108
In den Lüften schwellendes Gedröhne 120
In der Fremde 64
In der Frühe 82
In der Nacht, die die Bäume mit Blüten deckt 114
In der stillen Pracht 36
In einem kühlen Grunde 41
In Erinnerung 132
In mein gar zu dunkles Leben 47
Ins offne Fenster nickten 148

Kein Schlaf noch kühlt das Auge mir 82
Kennst du das Land, wo die Zitronen blühn 10
Klingling, bumbum und tschingdada 130

Lebewohl 85
„Lebe wohl!" — Du fühlest nicht 85
Leise zieht durch mein Gemüt 60

Lieblich war die Maiennacht 73
Lied des Türmers 17
Liederseelen 114
Liegt eine Stadt im Tale 140
Lob des Frühlings 26
Lucie 107

Mai 110
Mailied 2
Manche Nacht 142
Meine eingelegten Ruder triefen 124
Meine Mutter hat's gewollt 111
Meiner Mutter 135
Mein Liebchen, wir saßen beisammen 53
Mein liebes Mütterlein war verreist 75
Melde mir die Nachtgeräusche, Muse 115
Mignon 10
Mitternacht, die Gärten lauschen 138
Mondnacht 44
Morgenlied 24
Müde schleichen hier die Bäche 76

Nach einem Niederländer 123
Nach Frankreich zogen zwei Grenadier' 46
Nacht für Nacht 143
Nachtgefühl 92
Nachtgeräusche 115
Nacht ist wie ein stilles Meer 39
Nächtlich am Busento lispeln 66
Nachtlied 90
Nachts 35, 43
Neujahrsglocken 120
Nicht ein Flügelschlag ging durch die Welt 99
Noch ahnt man kaum der Sonne Licht 24
Noch unverrückt, o schöne Lampe 87
Normannenherzog Wilhelm sprach einmal 31
Nun ist es still um Hof und Scheuer 104

Oktoberlied 102
O mein Heimatland! O mein Vaterland 98

Quellende, schwellende Nacht.   90

Requiem   126
Rings ein Verstummen.   78

Saatengrün, Veilchenduft.   26
Säerspruch.   121
Sag, wo ist dein schönes Liebchen   58
Sah ein Knab' ein Röslein stehn   4
Schäfers Sonntagslied   22
Schaff', das Tagwerk meiner Hände   7
Schilflied   71
Schließe mir die Augen beide   113
Schnitterlied.   122
Schöne Junitage   138
Schön-Rohtraut   86
Schwer ist zu Gott der Abstieg   156
Sehet ihr am Fensterlein   83
Sehnsucht   40
Sein Blick ist vom Vorübergehn   153
Septembermorgen.   80
Sie saß so wie die anderen   154
Sommerbild.   96
Sommermittag.   104
Sommernacht   134
So stille ruht im Hafen   127
Still, es ist ein Tag   143
Stimme des Regens.   77

Täglich ging die wunderschöne   65
Taillefer   31
Tod in Ähren   131

Über allen Gipfeln.   6
Über die Heide   106
Über die Heide hallet mein Schritt   106
Um Mitternacht   79
Und frische Nahrung, neues Blut   3
Unter Sternen   101

Viererzug   137
Vom Himmel in die tiefsten Klüfte   103
Vor der Ernte   118
Vor der Türe schläft der Baum   136
Vorne vier nickende Pferdeköpfe.   137

Wandrers Nachtlied   5
Weihnachtslied   103
Weil' auf mir, du dunkles Auge   70
Welch ein Schwirren, welch ein Flug   20
Wem Gott will rechte Gunst erweisen   33
Wende dich, du kleiner Stern   101
Wenn der Regen   141
Wenn der uralte   16
Wenn die Felder   142
Wenn ich mich abends entkleide.   92
Wer hat dich, du schöner Wald   34
Wer nie sein Brot mit Tränen aß   11
Wer reitet so spät durch Nacht und Wind   14
Wer weiß wo   133
Widmung   156
Wiegenlied.   136
Wie heißt König Ringangs Töchterlein   86
Wie herrlich leuchtet   2
Wie oft sah ich die blassen Hände nähen   135
Wie rafft' ich mich auf in der Nacht   68
Wilde Rosen überschlugen   132
Willkommen und Abschied.   1
Willst du immer weiter schweifen   8
Winternacht   99
Wir haben ein Bett   139
Wir schnitten die Saaten, wir Buben und Dirnen   122
Wir schreiten auf und ab   149
Wir sind in trauer.   151
Wir träumten von einander   95

Zum Kampf der Wagen und Gesänge   18
Zum Sehen geboren   17
Zur Schmiede ging ein junger Held   27